Email :
Password: Tezmo0226@

True Stories 3

Sandra Heyer

True Stories: Level 3, Silver Edition

Pearson Education, 221 River Street, Hoboken, NJ 07030

Staff Credits: The people who made up the ***True Stories: Level 3, Silver Edition*** team, representing content creation, design, manufacturing, marketing, multimedia, project management, publishing, rights management, and testing, are Pietro Alongi, Tracey Cataldo, Dave Dickey, Warren Fischbach, Lucy Hart, Gosia Jaros-White, Barry Katzen, Linda Moser, Dana Pinter, Paula Van Ells, Joseph Vella, and Peter West.

Text design and layout: Don Williams
Composition: Page Designs International
Project supervision: Bernard Seal
Contributing editor: Bernard Seal

Cover images: *(from top to bottom)* Shyamalamuralinath/Shutterstock; Katelizabeth Photography/Alamy Stock Photo; Joel Sartore/National Geographic Creative/Alamy Stock Photo; Randy Duchaine/Alamy Stock Photo; majlan/Shutterstock; *(silver edition badge)* deepstock/Shutterstock.
Illustrations: Don Martinetti
Map: Page 66 Aptara

Library of Congress Cataloging-in-Publication Data

A catalog record for the print edition is available from the Library of Congress.

Printed in the United States of America

ISBN-10: 0-13-5177936
ISBN-13: 978-0-13-5177938

1 19

CONTENTS

Introduction iv
Acknowledgments vii
From the Author ix

UNIT 1 Puppy Love 2
UNIT 2 Surprise! It's Your Wedding! 6
UNIT 3 Bad News, Good News 10
UNIT 4 The Twins of Siam 14
UNIT 5 The Baby Exchange 18
UNIT 6 The Ghost 22
UNIT 7 The Way Home 26
UNIT 8 Everybody's Baby 30
UNIT 9 Pay It Forward 34
UNIT 10 Please Pass the Bird Brains 38
UNIT 11 Margaret Patrick...Meet Ruth Eisenberg . . . 42
UNIT 12 Finders Keepers? 46
UNIT 13 The Husband 50
UNIT 14 The Auction 54
UNIT 15 Money to Burn 58
UNIT 16 The School and the Stamp 62
UNIT 17 A Long Fishing Trip 66
UNIT 18 The Surgeon 70
UNIT 19 Customer Service? 74
UNIT 20 The Mermaid Balloon 78
UNIT 21 The Two Lives of Mary Sutton 82
UNIT 22 Two Strangers 86

Answer Key 91
Credits 104

INTRODUCTION

TRUE STORIES, SILVER EDITION

The Silver Edition of *True Stories* is a five-level reading series. The series is appropriate for beginning to high-intermediate learners of English as a Second or Foreign Language. The Silver Edition consists of revised editions of six of the highly successful and popular *True Stories in the News* books that have provided entertaining stories and effective reading skill instruction for many years. In fact, the first book in that series was published over twenty-five years ago (hence the title "Silver" Edition). The *True Stories* series has been going strong ever since.

NEW IN THE SILVER EDITION

- **New and updated stories.** Some stories have been updated, and some have been replaced with fresh new readings that have been thoroughly classroom-tested before making it into print. All of the readings that have proven to be favorites of students and teachers over the years have been retained.
- **A colorful new design.** Originally published solely in black and white, the new edition has a new full-color design with colorful new photos. The color design makes the readings even more inviting, and the color photos that accompany the readings enhance understanding and enjoyment of the stories.
- **A uniform unit structure.** The books in the series have been given a consistent unit structure that runs across all six books. This predictable structure makes it easy for teachers to teach the series at different levels and for students to progress seamlessly from one level to the next.
- **Audio recordings of every reading.** Every story in the series has been recorded and made available online for students or teachers to download.
- **Online Answer Keys and To the Teacher notes.** In addition to being in the back of the books, as they were in the previous editions, the Answer Keys are now also online as downloadable pdfs. The To the Teacher notes that were previously in the back of the books, however, are now only online. This section provides additional information about the stories and teaching tips. Additional practice activities are also now available online.

THE APPROACH

The underlying premise in this series has always been that when second language learners are engaged in a pleasurable reading experience in the second language, then language learning will take place effortlessly and effectively. The formula is simple: Offer students a true story that fascinates and surprises them. Have them read and enjoy the story. Focus their attention on some useful vocabulary in the story. Confirm that they fully understand the story with reading comprehension exercises. Develop reading skills that progress from basic to more complex. Finally, use the content and the topic of the story to engage in discussion and writing tasks, from tightly structured to more open-ended.

UNIT COMPONENTS

Pre-Reading

Each unit begins with a pre-reading task that piques students' curiosity about the content of the story. Students' attention is drawn to the art that accompanies the reading and the title of the reading as they predict what the story is going to be about.

Reading

The readings are short enough to be read by the students in class; at the lower levels, the stories can be read in minutes. As the levels become higher, the readings do become longer and more challenging. Still, even at the highest levels, each reading and the exercises immediately following it can be completed in one class meeting.

Post-Reading

While there is some variation in the post-reading activities, the following are in all six books:

- **Vocabulary.** Useful key vocabulary items are selected from the readings for presentation and practice. The vocabulary activities vary from unit to unit, and the number of vocabulary items and the extent of the practice increases from level to level.
- **Comprehension.** At least two different comprehension tasks follow the vocabulary section. The exercises have descriptive titles, such as Understanding the Main Ideas, Remembering Details, or Understanding Cause and Effect, so that teachers and students know which cognitive skills are being applied. The exercises have a great deal of variety, keeping students engaged and motivated.
- **Discussion.** Having read and studied the stories, students are encouraged to discuss some aspect arising from the story. Even at the lowest level, students are given simple tasks that will give them the opportunity to talk in pairs, in small groups, or as a whole class.
- **Writing.** The final section of each unit has students produce a short piece of writing related to the reading. Often the writing task derives directly from the Discussion, in which case the title of the section is Discussion/Writing. The writing tasks are level-appropriate and vary in complexity depending on student proficiency. The tasks are not intended to be graded. They simply provide a final opportunity for students to engage with the topic of the reading and deepen their understanding and enjoyment of the story.

TRUE STORIES, LEVEL 3

True Stories, Level 3 is the fourth book in the Silver Edition of the *True Stories* series. It is intended for low-intermediate learners of English. It consists of 22 four-page units, each with the following distinguishing features:

- The pre-reading task has students look at a photo that prompts them to speculate on the content of the story.
- Each story has an average length of 475 words.
- The stories are told in the simple past, past progressive, and future tenses.
- Writing exercises require students to fill in a chart, complete sentences, compose single sentences, or write a short paragraph.

ACKNOWLEDGMENTS

I would like to thank

- the many teachers whose invaluable feedback helped me assess how the stories and exercises were working outside the small sphere of my own classroom. If I were to list you all by name, this acknowledgments section would go on for pages. I would like to thank three colleagues in particular: legendary teacher Peggy Miles, who introduced me to the world of English language teaching; Sharron Bassano, whose innovative techniques for teaching beginning-level students informed my own approach; and Jorge Islas Martinez, whose enthusiasm and dedication remain a constant inspiration;
- my students, who shared personal stories that became the examples for the discussion and writing exercises;
- the people in the stories who supplied details that were not in news sources: Twyla Thompson, John Koehler, Dorothy Peckham, Chi Hsii Tsui, Margaret Patrick, Trish Moore and Rhonda Gill (grandmother and mother of Desiree), Friendship Force participants, Natalie Garibian, Mirsada Buric, and the late Irvin Scott;
- the teachers and editors who made important contributions at different stages of development to the previous editions of these books and whose influence can still be seen throughout this new edition: Allen Ascher, John Barnes, Karen Davy, Joanne Dresner, Nancy Hayward, Stacey Hunter, Penny LaPorte, Laura LeDrean, Françoise Leffler, Linda Moser, Dana Klinek Pinter, Mary Perrotta Rich, Debbie Sistino, and Paula Van Ells;
- Rachel Hayward and Megan Hohenstein, who assisted in piloting and researching new material for the Silver Edition;
- the team at Pearson, whose experienced hands skillfully put together all the moving pieces in the preparation of this Silver Edition: Pietro Alongi, Tracey Cataldo, Warren Fischbach, Lucy Hart, Gosia Jaros-White, Linda Moser, Dana Pinter, Joseph Vella, and Peter West;
- copyeditor and fact checker, Kate Smyres; and proofreader, Ann Dickson;
- editor extraordinaire Françoise Leffler, who lent her expertise to *True Stories* levels 4 and 5;
- Bernard Seal at Page Designs International, who guided this project from start to finish with dedication, creativity, pragmatism, and the occasional “crazy”—but brilliant—idea;
- Don Williams at Page Designs International, whose talent for design is evident on every page; and
- my husband, John Hajdu Heyer, who read the first draft of every story I’ve considered for the *True Stories* series. The expression on his face as he read told me whether or not the story was a keeper. He didn’t know that. Now he does.

FROM THE AUTHOR

Dear Teachers and Students,

This new edition of *True Stories* is the Silver Edition because it celebrates an anniversary—it has been more than 25 years since the first *True Stories* book was published. The way we get our news has changed a lot over the years, but some things have remained the same: Fascinating stories are in the news every day, and the goal of the *True Stories* series is still to bring the best of them to you.

The question students ask most often about these stories is *Are they true?* The answer is *yes*—to the best of my knowledge, these stories are true. I've fact-checked stories by contacting reporters, photojournalists, and research librarians all over the world. I've even called some of the people in the stories to be sure I have the facts right.

Once I'm as sure as I can be that a story is true, the story has to pass one more test. My students read the story, and after they finish reading, they give each story one, two, or three stars. They take this responsibility seriously; they know that only the top-rated stories will become part of the *True Stories* reading series.

I hope that you, too, think these are three-star stories. And I hope that reading them encourages you to share your own stories, which are always the most amazing true stories of all.

Sandra Heyer

UNIT 1

1 PRE-READING

A **Look at the picture. Answer the questions.**

1. Do you think dogs can love people?
2. Do you think dogs can love other dogs?

B **Read the title of the story. Look at the picture again. Answer the questions.**

1. What do you think this story is about?
2. Can you guess what happens?

Puppy Love

"Shiro! Shiro!"

Mr. and Mrs. Nakamura were worried. Their dog, Shiro, was missing. "Shiro!" they called again and again. Mr. and Mrs. Nakamura lived on a small island in Japan. They looked everywhere on the island, but they couldn't find Shiro.

The next day, Mr. Nakamura heard a noise at the front door. He opened the door, and there was Shiro. Shiro was very wet, and he was shivering.

A few days later, Shiro disappeared again. He disappeared in the morning, and he came back late at night. When he came back, he was wet and shivering.

Shiro began to disappear often. He always disappeared in the morning and came back late at night. He was always wet when he came back.

Mr. Nakamura was curious. "Where does Shiro go?" he wondered. "Why is he wet when he comes back?"

One morning Mr. Nakamura followed Shiro.

Shiro walked to the beach, ran into the water, and began to swim. Mr. Nakamura jumped into his boat and followed his dog. Shiro swam for about two miles (3.2 kilometers). Then he was tired, so he climbed onto a rock and rested. A few minutes later, he jumped back into the water and continued swimming.

Shiro swam for three hours. Then he arrived at an island. He walked onto the beach, shook the water off, and walked toward town. Mr. Nakamura followed him. Shiro walked to a house. A dog was waiting in front of the house. Shiro ran to the dog, and the two dogs began to play. The dog's name was Marilyn. Marilyn was Shiro's girlfriend.

Marilyn lived on Zamami, another Japanese island. Shiro and the Nakamuras used to live on Zamami. Then the Nakamuras moved to Aka, a smaller island. They took Shiro with them. Shiro missed Marilyn very much and wanted to be with her. But he wanted to be with the Nakamuras, too. So, Shiro lived with the Nakamuras on the island of Aka and swam to Zamami to visit Marilyn.

People were amazed when they heard about Shiro. The distance from Aka to Zamami is two and a half miles (4 kilometers), and the ocean between the islands is very rough. "Nobody can swim from Aka to Zamami!" the people said.

Shiro became famous. Many people went to Zamami because they wanted to see Shiro. During one Japanese holiday, 3,000 people visited Zamami. They waited on the beach for Shiro. "Maybe Shiro will swim to Zamami today," they said. They all wanted to see Shiro, the dog who was in love.

2 VOCABULARY

Complete the sentences with the words below.

amazed	curious	missing	rough	shivering

1. Shiro disappeared. The Nakamuras looked everywhere for him, but they couldn't find him. Their dog was ___missing___.
2. Shiro always came back at night. He was wet and cold, so he was ______________.
3. "Where does Shiro go?" Mr. Nakamura wondered. He wanted to know. One day he followed his dog because he was ______________.
4. Shiro's swimming surprised people. "Nobody can swim from Aka to Zamami!" they said. People were ______________ when they heard about Shiro.
5. It was difficult for Shiro to swim because the ocean was ______________.

3 COMPREHENSION

UNDERSTANDING THE MAIN IDEAS

Circle the letter of the best answer.

1. "Puppy Love" is about
   a. two islands in Japan.
   b. a Japanese holiday.
   c. a dog who visits his girlfriend.
2. People were amazed when they heard about Shiro because
   a. dogs don't usually fall in love.
   b. swimming from Aka to Zamami is very difficult.
   c. Shiro is an unusual name for a dog.

UNDERSTANDING CAUSE AND EFFECT

Find the best way to complete each sentence. Write the letter of the answer on the line.

1. Mr. and Mrs. Nakamura were worried __c__
2. Shiro was always wet when he came back _____
3. Mr. Nakamura followed Shiro _____
4. Shiro swam to Zamami _____
5. Three thousand people went to Zamami _____

a. because his girlfriend lived there.
b. because he was curious.
c. because their dog was missing.
d. because he swam in the ocean.
e. because they wanted to see Shiro.

REVIEWING THE STORY

Write the missing words. Then read the story again and check your answers.

Mr. Nakamura was curious about his dog, Shiro. Shiro often __disappeared__ (1.) in the morning and ________ (2.) back late at night. He ________ (3.) always wet when he came back.

One morning Mr. Nakamura ________ (4.) Shiro. Shiro walked to the beach, ran into the water, and began to ________ (5.). He swam to Zamami, a Japanese island. Marilyn lived on Zamami. Marilyn was Shiro's ________ (6.).

People were amazed when they heard ________ (7.) Shiro. The ________ (8.) from Aka to Zamami is two and a half miles, and the ocean between the islands is very ________ (9.).

Shiro became ________ (10.). Many people went to Zamami because they wanted to see Shiro, the dog who was in ________ (11.).

4 DISCUSSION / WRITING

Shiro is the Nakamuras' pet. Shiro does something unusual. He swims two and a half miles to visit his "girlfriend."

A **Interview a classmate who has a pet. Ask your classmate the questions below. Listen carefully and write your classmate's answers.**

1. What kind of pet do you have?

    ____

2. What is your pet's name?

    ____

3. How old is your pet?

    ____

4. Is your pet smart like Shiro?

    ____

5. Does your pet do anything unusual?

    ____

6. What do you like to do with your pet?

    ____

7. Do you want more pets?

    ____

B **Tell the class what you learned about your classmate's pet.**

C **Use your classmate's answers to write a paragraph on your own paper. Here is what one student wrote.**

Irma has a pet goldfish. His name is Tiger, and he is about one year old. Irma named her fish Tiger because he has stripes like a tiger. Tiger is not smart like Shiro. Tiger doesn't do anything unusual. He just swims around in his goldfish bowl. Maybe Irma will buy another goldfish. Then Tiger will have a friend.

UNIT 2

1 PRE-READING

A **Look at the picture. Answer the questions.**

1. What is the woman doing?
2. Where do you think this is?
3. How do you think the woman feels? How do you think the man feels?

B **Read the title of the story. Look at the picture again. Answer the questions.**

1. What do you think this story is about?
2. Can you guess what happens?

Surprise! It's Your Wedding!

"Good night, John."

"Good night, Lynn."

Lynn Millington kissed her boyfriend good night. He walked to his car and drove away. Lynn walked into her house. It was midnight. Her parents were sleeping, and the house was quiet. Lynn sat down on the sofa. She had a problem, and she needed some time to think.

Lynn's boyfriend was John Biggin. John loved Lynn, and Lynn loved John. They were very happy together. What was the problem? Lynn wanted to get married. John wanted to get married, too, but he was afraid.

Sometimes Lynn and John talked about getting married. "Let's get married in June," Lynn said. "June is a beautiful month for a wedding."

"June?" John asked. "This June? Let's not get married in June. Let's wait a little longer."

Lynn waited…and waited. She was very patient. She was patient, but she wanted to get married. Lynn's parents wanted her to get married, too; they liked John. John's parents also wanted them to get married because they liked Lynn. Suddenly Lynn had an idea. "John's parents will help me!" she thought.

The next morning, Lynn called John's parents. "I need your help," Lynn told them. "John wants to get married, but he's afraid. Let's plan a wedding for John and me. It will be this Saturday. Invite your family. But don't tell John about the wedding."

Next, Lynn called Bob Rapper. Bob was John's best friend. "I need your help," Lynn told Bob. "Tell John that you're getting married this Saturday. Invite him to your wedding."

Bob wasn't really getting married on Saturday. It was a trick. John and Lynn were getting married on Saturday, but John didn't know it.

On Saturday morning, John put on his best suit. Then he drove to the courthouse in Bridlington, England. He walked into the courthouse and looked around. He saw his friend Bob. He saw his girlfriend, Lynn. Then he saw his parents, relatives, and friends. He saw Lynn's family and friends. Suddenly John understood. This was not Bob's wedding! This was John's wedding! John began to shake, but he didn't run away. Twenty minutes later, John and Lynn were husband and wife.

After the wedding, a photographer took pictures of John and Lynn. In every picture, John is smiling. Lynn, of course, is smiling, too.

2 VOCABULARY

Complete the sentences with the words below.

courthouse   patient   shake   trick   wedding

1. Lynn waited and waited. She was very ___patient___.
2. John's best friend, Bob, told him, "I'm getting married on Saturday." That wasn't true; Bob wasn't really getting married. It was a ______________.
3. John and Lynn live in England. In England some people get married at a ______________.
4. When John saw his friends and family, he got nervous. His body began to ______________.
5. Lynn and John got married. After the ______________, a photographer took pictures.

3 COMPREHENSION

UNDERSTANDING THE MAIN IDEAS

Circle the letter of the best answer.

1. What was Lynn's problem?
   a. John's parents didn't like her.
   b. Lynn loved John's best friend.
   c. John was afraid to get married.
2. John and Lynn's wedding was unusual because
   a. Lynn didn't wear a white dress.
   b. John didn't know about the wedding.
   c. the wedding was at a courthouse.

UNDERSTANDING CONNECTIONS

Find the best way to complete each sentence. Write the letter of the answer on the line.

1. John wanted to get married, but b
2. Lynn was patient, but _____
3. Lynn told John's parents, "Invite your family to the wedding, but _____
4. When John understood that it was his wedding, he began to shake, but _____

a. don't tell John."
b. he was afraid.
c. he didn't run away.
d. she wanted to get married.

REMEMBERING DETAILS

One word in each sentence is not correct. Find the word and cross it out. Write the correct word.

1. John loved Lynn and wanted to get married, but he was ~~angry.~~ afraid
2. Lynn told John's brothers, "I need your help."
3. "Let's plan a party for John and me," Lynn told John's parents.
4. Next, Lynn called Bob, who was John's boss.
5. She told him, "Tell John that you're getting married this Monday, and invite him to the wedding."
6. Bob wasn't really getting married; it was a problem.
7. On Saturday morning, John put on his best suit and drove to the library in Bridlington, England.

8. At the courthouse, he called Lynn, his friends, and his relatives.

9. Suddenly he understood: This was Bob's wedding!

10. Twenty minutes later, John and Lynn were boyfriend and wife.

4 DISCUSSION

A **Read the sentences and check (✓) *YES* or *NO*.**

	YES	NO
1. I think John is happy that he married Lynn.	☐	☐
2. Lynn tricked John. I think that was a good idea.	☐	☐
3. I think John and Lynn will have a long and happy marriage.	☐	☐
4. John is 24 years old. That is a good age for a man to get married.	☐	☐
5. I am (I was) afraid to get married.	☐	☐

B **Read the sentences and your answers to a partner. Explain your answers.**

5 WRITING

A **Is it better to be married or single? Fill in the chart below.**

It is better to be married. Why?	It is better to be single. Why?
1. ______	1. ______
2. ______	2. ______
3. ______	3. ______

B **Discuss your answers with your classmates.**

UNIT 3

1 PRE-READING

A Look at the picture. Answer the questions.

1. What kinds of bad news do people sometimes get from a doctor?
2. What do they do after they get the bad news?

B Read the title of the story. Look at the picture again. Answer the questions.

1. What do you think the man's bad news was?
2. What do you think his good news was?
3. What do you think this story is about?
4. Can you guess what happens?

Bad News, Good News

John Brandrick had a terrible pain in his stomach, so he went to his doctor. The doctor sent him to the hospital for tests and then told him the bad news. "Mr. Brandrick, you are a very sick man," the doctor said. "You have only six months to live."

"Isn't there anything you can do?" John asked the doctor. "Medicine? Surgery?"

"I'm sorry," the doctor answered. "There's nothing we can do. Enjoy the time you have left. I'm very, very sorry."

John was 62 years old. He was divorced and had two grown children. He told his children the bad news. Then he told Sally, his girlfriend. "Let's not be sad," he told them. "The doctor told me, 'Enjoy the time you have left.' That's what we're going to do. We're going to enjoy every minute of the rest of my life."

The next day, John quit his job. He had $23,000 in savings, and he decided to spend it. John and Sally lived on the coast of England, in a beautiful area where tourists often visit. John and Sally took short trips along the coast and ate at all the best restaurants. John bought expensive gifts for his family and friends.

All spring and summer, John spent his money. When fall came, he began thinking about his death. "What will my family do with all my things after I die?" he wondered. "I'll sell my things now so my family won't have to."

John sold most of his furniture. Then he sold his car. "I won't need my winter clothes," he thought, "because I won't be alive this winter." He gave all his winter clothes away. He kept only a black suit, a white shirt, and a red tie. "Bury me in that suit," he told Sally.

Fall came and went. Winter came and went. Spring came again, and John was still alive. He went back to his doctor.

"How's the stomach pain?" the doctor asked.

"It's gone," John said.

The doctor sent John to the hospital for tests and then told him the good news. "You are in perfect health," the doctor said.

"So I'm not going to die soon?" John asked.

"No," the doctor said. "I think you're fine."

"But what about the tests I had at the hospital a year ago?" John asked.

"I don't know," the doctor said. "Maybe there was a mistake."

John told Sally and his children the good news, and they had a big celebration. But later John thought, "I'm going to live. But how am I going to live with no job, no furniture, no car, no warm clothes, and no money?"

John wants the hospital to pay him for its mistake. So he is going to court. He wants the hospital to give him money for new furniture, a new car, and new clothes. He also wants the hospital to put $23,000 in his savings account. A judge will decide if the hospital has to give John money. John is hoping the judge will give him more good news.

2 VOCABULARY

Which words have the same meaning as the words in *italics*? Write the letter of the answer on the line.

e 1. John had two *grown* children.

_____ 2. "Enjoy *the time you have left*," the doctor said.

_____ 3. "*Let's not* be sad," John told his family.

_____ 4. John had $23,000 in his *savings*.

_____ 5. John and his family had a *celebration*.

a. I don't want us to

b. party

c. the days you have until you die

d. bank account

e. adult

3 COMPREHENSION

UNDERSTANDING THE MAIN IDEAS

There are two correct ways to complete each sentence. Circle the letters of the *two* correct answers.

1. John's doctor told him,
   a. "You are a very sick man."
   b. "You have a bad heart."
   c. "You have only six months to live."
2. When John asked his doctor, "Isn't there anything you can do?" the doctor answered,
   a. "We can try surgery."
   b. "There's nothing we can do."
   c. "I'm very, very sorry."
3. John wanted to enjoy the time he had left, so he
   a. quit his job.
   b. married his girlfriend, Sally.
   c. spent his savings.
4. John decided to sell
   a. most of his furniture.
   b. his car.
   c. his house.
5. When John returned to his doctor one year later, the doctor told him,
   a. "You are in perfect health."
   b. "Maybe the hospital made a mistake."
   c. "You should go to court."
6. John wants the hospital to
   a. give money to Sally and his children.
   b. give him money for new furniture, a new car, and new clothes.
   c. give him $23,000 for his savings account.

FINDING INFORMATION

Read each question. Find the answer in the paragraphs on the next page and circle it. Write the number of the question above the answer.

1. How old was John?
2. How many children did he have?
3. What was his girlfriend's name?
4. When did John quit his job?
5. How much money did John have in savings?
6. Where did John and Sally live?
7. Where did they eat?
8. What did John buy?

John was 62 years old. He was divorced and had two grown children. He told his children the bad news. Then he told Sally, his girlfriend. "Let's not be sad," he told them. "Let's enjoy the time I have left."

The next day, John quit his job. He had $23,000 in savings, and he decided to spend it. John and Sally lived on the coast of England, in a beautiful area where tourists often visit. John and Sally took short trips along the coast and ate at all the best restaurants. John bought expensive gifts for his family and friends.

UNDERSTANDING A SUMMARY

Imagine this: You want to tell the story "Bad News, Good News" to a friend. You want to tell the story quickly, in only four sentences. Which four sentences tell the story best? Check (✓) your answer.

☐ **1.** John Brandrick had terrible stomach pains, so he went to his doctor. After John had some tests at the hospital, his doctor told him he had only six months to live. John has two grown children and a girlfriend named Sally. He wanted to enjoy the rest of his life with Sally and his children, so he quit his job and spent all his savings.

☐ **2.** John Brandrick's doctor sent him to the hospital for tests and then told him he was going to die. So John quit his job, spent his savings, sold his car and most of his furniture, and gave away his winter clothes. But the tests were wrong; John is not going to die. John wants the hospital to pay him for its mistake.

4 DISCUSSION / WRITING

John wants the hospital to pay him for its mistake. He wants money for new furniture, a new car, and new clothes. He also wants $23,000 for his savings account.

A **Do you think the hospital should pay John? Check (✓) your answer. Then complete the sentence you checked.**

☐ No, I don't think the hospital should pay John because ______________________________

____.

☐ Yes, I think the hospital should pay John $__________ because ______________________

____.

B **Explain your answer in a small group.**

UNIT 4

Chang and Eng, Siamese Twins

1 PRE-READING

A Look at the picture. Answer the questions.

1. The men in the photo are the famous Twins of Siam. How old do you think the photo is?
2. What is unusual about these men?

B Read the title of the story. Look at the picture again. Answer the questions.

1. What do you think this story is about?
2. Can you guess what happens?

The Twins of Siam

A young mother was lying on a bed. She had just given birth to twin boys. She was tired but happy. A woman was helping her. Suddenly the woman screamed. "What's the matter?" the mother cried. She lifted her head and looked at her babies. The babies were joined at their chests. She could not separate them.

That happened in Siam—now called Thailand—in 1811. The mother named her babies Chang and Eng. Chang and Eng grew up and became the famous Siamese twins.

People came from all over Siam to stare at the twins. One day, when the twins were 18, an American saw them. He thought, "I can make money with the twins." He asked Chang and Eng, "Will you come with me to the United States?" Chang and Eng wanted to go to the United States, so they went with the man. They never saw Siam or their family again.

Chang and Eng traveled with the American for ten years. Later they traveled alone. People paid to see them and ask them questions about their lives. Finally, the twins got tired of traveling. They got tired of answering questions. They decided to live quietly in North Carolina.

Soon after they moved to North Carolina, the twins met two sisters. The sisters' names were Adelaide and Sarah. The twins fell in love with the sisters. Chang married Adelaide, and Eng married Sarah. The marriages were very unusual. Adelaide and Sarah lived in separate houses. The twins lived in one house for four days. Then they went to the other house for four days. The marriages were unusual, but they were long and happy. Chang and Adelaide had ten children, and Eng and Sarah had eleven children.

The twins were happy with Adelaide and Sarah, but they were not always happy with each other. Sometimes they argued, and they didn't talk to each other. They asked doctor after doctor, "Please separate us." Every doctor said, "I can't separate you. The operation is too dangerous." So, the twins stayed joined together.

One night, when the twins were 63, Eng suddenly woke up. He looked at Chang, who was lying beside him. Chang was not breathing. Eng screamed for help, and one of his sons came.

"Uncle Chang is dead," the young man said.

"Then I am going to die, too," Eng said, and he began to cry. Two hours later, Eng was dead.

For 63 years, the twins of Siam lived together as one. In the end, they also died as one.

2 VOCABULARY

Complete the sentences with the words below.

argued got tired joined stare

1. The twins were together, and their mother couldn't separate them. They were ____joined____ at their chests.
2. People looked at Chang and Eng because the twins were unusual. People came from all over Siam to ________________ at them.
3. After traveling for many years, the twins didn't want to travel anymore. They ________________ of it.
4. Sometimes the twins spoke in angry voices. They ________________ because they were not happy with each other.

3 COMPREHENSION

UNDERSTANDING THE MAIN IDEAS

Circle the letter of the best answer.

1. This story is about
   a. dangerous operations.
   b. unusual marriages.
   c. Siamese twin brothers.
2. The twins talked to many doctors because
   a. the twins were often sick.
   b. they wanted the doctors to separate them.
   c. the doctors wanted to study the twins.

REMEMBERING DETAILS

One word in each sentence is not correct. Find the word and cross it out. Write the correct word.

1. The story happened in Siam—now called ~~China~~ Thailand—in 1811.
2. Chang and Eng grew up and became the famous Siamese doctors.
3. People came from all over Siam to laugh at the twins.
4. An Australian asked Chang and Eng to come with him to the United States.
5. Chang and Eng traveled with the American for ten days.
6. After they moved to North Carolina, the twins met two cousins.
7. The marriages were unusual, but they were long and unhappy.
8. Every doctor said, "I can separate you because the operation is too dangerous."

UNDERSTANDING REASONS

Find the best way to complete each sentence. Write the letter of the answer on the line.

1. The young mother lifted her head e
2. Chang and Eng went to the United States _____
3. People paid _____
4. The twins moved to North Carolina _____
5. The twins went to doctor after doctor _____

a. to live quietly.
b. to ask the twins questions.
c. to ask about an operation.
d. to travel with the American.
e. to look at her babies.

4 DISCUSSION

The twins of Siam were famous. People paid to see them and ask them questions about their lives.

Think of a famous person, living or dead. Tell your teacher who you are thinking of, but don't tell your classmates. Then sit in front of the class. Your classmates will ask you questions, and you will answer only "yes" or "no." Can your classmates guess who you are? Here are some sample questions.

- Are you a woman?
- Are you alive?
- Are you an actor?
- Are you rich?
- Did you live a long time ago?
- Are you a political leader?
- Are you French?
- Are you an athlete?
- Are you a singer?
- Are you handsome?

5 WRITING

The twins married two sisters. Their marriages were happy. Not all marriages are happy every day.

A **Look at this picture of a husband and wife. Why is the husband angry? What is he saying? Write it.**

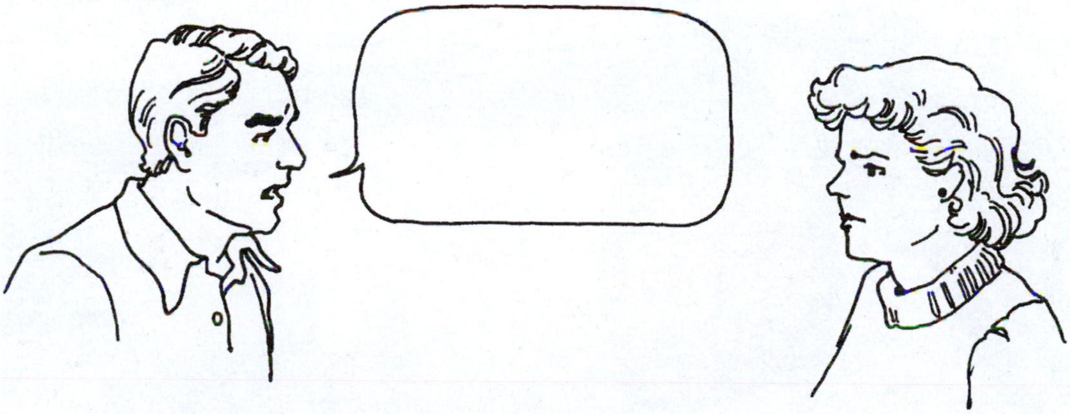

B **Look at the next picture. Why is the wife angry? What is she saying? Write it.**

C **What did you write? Tell your classmates.**

UNIT 5

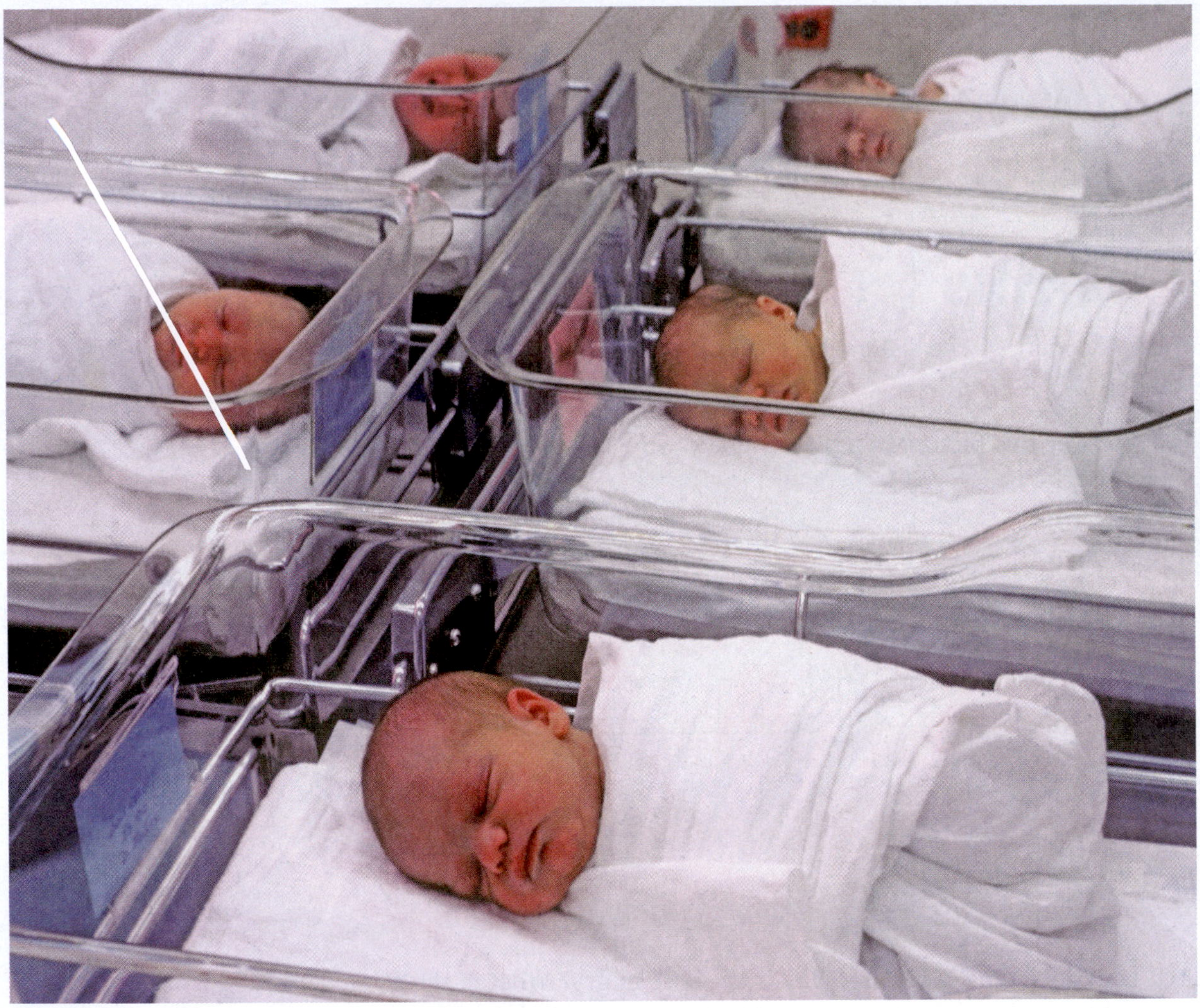

1 PRE-READING

A Look at the picture. Answer the questions.

1. How old are the babies?
2. Where is this?
3. What mistakes can happen here?

B Read the title of the story. Look at the picture again. Answer the questions.

1. What do you think this story is about?
2. Can you guess what happens?

The Baby Exchange

Selma Scarausi looked at her baby daughter and smiled. The baby smiled back. Selma began to cry. "I love my baby very much," Selma thought. "But is she really my baby?"

Selma's baby was born at a hospital in São Paulo, Brazil. A few days later, Selma and the baby came home from the hospital. Friends and relatives were surprised when they saw the baby. The baby didn't look like her parents. The baby had dark skin and curly hair, but Selma and her husband had light skin and straight hair. "Babies change," everyone thought. "She will look like her parents when she is older."

But the baby didn't change. When she was nine months old, she still looked very different from her parents. Selma and her husband Paulo took the baby back to the hospital. "Are you sure this is our baby?" they asked the hospital director.

"Of course she is your baby," the director said. "Immediately after the babies are born, we give them bracelets with numbers. Your baby was number 51. You left the hospital with baby 51. A mistake is impossible."

"A mistake is possible," Selma and Paulo thought. "We have another family's baby. And somewhere another family has our baby. But São Paulo is a city of seven million people. How can we find our baby?"

Selma and Paulo went to the hospital again. A nurse at the hospital told Paulo, "I remember another couple. Their baby didn't look like them. The parents had dark skin, but the baby had light skin. The father had very curly hair, but the baby had straight hair." The nurse gave Paulo the couple's address.

The next day, Selma took her baby to the couple's house. She knocked, and a woman opened the door. The woman took one look at Selma's baby and fainted. Selma helped her into the house. There, in the living room, was a nine-month-old baby. Selma knew that the baby was hers.

Selma and Paulo's baby was living with Maria and Luiz Souza. The Souzas also had wondered about their baby because she looked so different from them. When Maria Souza saw the baby in Selma's arms, she, too, knew the baby was hers.

The hospital made a mistake. Both babies were born at the hospital on the same day. The hospital gave both babies the number 51.

During the next weeks, the two families prepared to exchange babies. First, they exchanged information about the babies' habits. Then they exchanged toys and clothes. Finally, with smiles and tears, they exchanged babies.

2 VOCABULARY

Which picture or words have the same meaning as the words in *italics*? Circle the letter of the answer.

1. The hospital gave the babies *bracelets* with numbers.

   (a.) 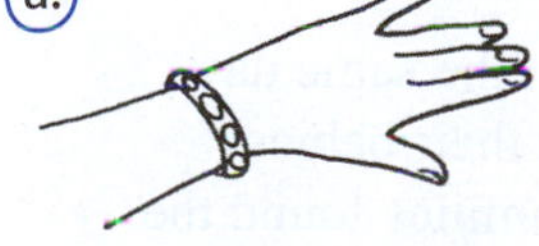

   b. 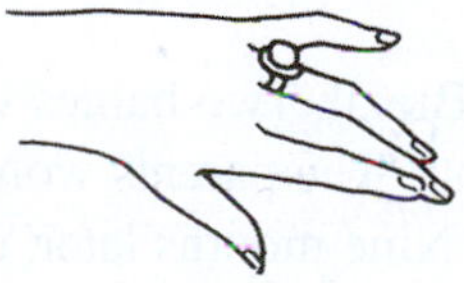

2. Maria Souza took one look at Selma's baby and *fainted*.
   a. left the house with the baby
   b. fell to the floor and didn't move
3. The two families exchanged information about the babies' *habits*.
   a. things people do every day
   b. places people like to go
4. Finally, with smiles and *tears*, they exchanged babies.
   a. water that comes from people's eyes when they cry
   b. gifts that people give to babies

3 COMPREHENSION

UNDERSTANDING THE MAIN IDEAS

Circle the letter of the best answer.

1. The story is about
   a. the city of São Paulo, Brazil.
   b. two couples who got the wrong babies.
   c. babies' habits, toys, and clothes.
2. Selma and Paulo thought, "We have the wrong baby" because
   a. hospitals sometimes make mistakes.
   b. they wanted a son, not a daughter.
   c. their baby didn't look like them.
3. Selma and Paulo found their baby with the help of
   a. a nurse at the hospital.
   b. the director of the hospital.
   c. Maria and Louiz Souza.

UNDERSTANDING CAUSE AND EFFECT

Find the best way to complete each sentence. Write the letter of the answer on the line.

1. Friends and relatives were surprised _e_
2. Selma and Paulo went back to the hospital ____
3. The hospital director said that a mistake was impossible ____
4. It was difficult for Selma and Paulo to find their baby ____
5. Maria Souza fainted ____

a. because São Paulo is a big city.
b. because she knew that the baby in Selma's arms was her baby.
c. because they thought they had the wrong baby.
d. because the hospital gave each baby a number.
e. because the baby didn't look like her parents.

UNDERSTANDING A SUMMARY

Imagine this: You want to tell the story "The Baby Exchange" to a friend. You want to tell the story quickly, in only four sentences. Which four sentences tell the story best? Check (✓) your answer.

☐ 1. There was a mistake at a hospital in Brazil. Two babies were born on the same day and went home with the wrong parents. The parents wondered about their babies because the babies didn't look them. Nine months later, one of the families found the other family, and the two families exchanged babies.

☐ 2. A Brazilian woman had a baby at a hospital in São Paulo. She wondered about her baby because the baby didn't look like her or her husband. When the baby was nine months old, the woman and her husband took their baby to the hospital. They asked the hospital director, "Are you sure this is our baby?"

4 DISCUSSION / WRITING

Before the families exchanged babies, they exchanged information about the babies' habits.

A **Find out about your classmates' habits. Choose one of the questions below. (Each student must choose a different question.) Ask everyone in the class your question. Make a note of how many people answered *Yes*, *No*, or *Sometimes*.**

1. Do you sleep in the afternoon?
2. Do you sing in the shower?
3. Do you exercise?
4. Do you bite your nails?
5. Do you come to class late?
6. Do you walk fast?
7. Do you eat late at night?
8. Do you go to bed after midnight?
9. Do you read before you go to sleep?
10. Do you sleep with two pillows?
11. Do you drink coffee in the morning?
12. Do you eat breakfast?
13. Do you make your bed every day?
14. Do you listen to loud music when you study?
15. Do you play games on your phone?

YES

NO

SOMETIMES

B **Write a summary of what you learned about your classmates' habits. For example:**

Only four people always sleep in the afternoon. Two people sometimes sleep in the afternoon. The rest of the class never sleeps in the afternoon.

____

____

____

____

____

____

C **Read your summary aloud to the class.**

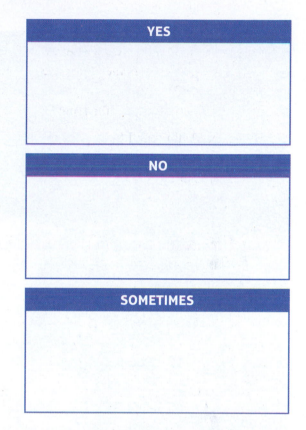

UNIT 6

1 PRE-READING

A **Look at the picture. Answer the questions.**

1. What time is it?
2. Why can't people sometimes sleep at night?

B **Read the title of the story. Look at the picture again. Answer the questions.**

1. What do you think this story is about?
2. Can you guess what happens?

The Ghost

One night at 2 a.m., Alfred Mansbridge heard something and woke up. He sat up in bed and listened. Someone was speaking in a quiet voice. It sounded like a child... or maybe a ghost.

Alfred was a 69-year-old widower, and he lived alone. He looked around his bedroom. There was nobody there.

"Maybe I was dreaming," Alfred thought. He went back to sleep.

The next night at 2 a.m., Alfred heard the quiet voice again. He sat up in bed and listened carefully. "Come and catch me," the voice said. It repeated the sentence five times. Then it was silent. That night Alfred lay awake for a long time.

For the next three months, Alfred heard the quiet voice every night at 2 a.m. "Come and catch me," it repeated for 15 seconds. Sometimes Alfred got up and searched his apartment, but he never found anyone or anything. He began to have trouble sleeping. Some nights he didn't sleep at all.

One day, Alfred's daughter and seven-year-old grandson came to visit. "Dad, are you okay?" his daughter asked. "You look tired."

"I *am* tired," Alfred told her. "Every night at 2 a.m., a quiet voice wakes me up. It says, 'Come and catch me.' I'm having trouble sleeping."

"I'm worried about you," his daughter said. "I think you're alone too much."

"My daughter thinks I'm crazy," Alfred thought. "But I'm not crazy; the voice is real! It's not a ghost—I don't believe in ghosts. So who is speaking to me every night? This is a real mystery, and I'm going to solve it."

The next day, Alfred bought a tape recorder. At 2 a.m., he recorded the quiet voice. Then he played the recording for his daughter. She immediately called the police. "Someone—or something—is in my father's apartment!" she told the police.

That night two police officers came to Alfred's apartment. One police officer sat in the kitchen, and the other sat in the living room. Alfred was in the bedroom. At 2 a.m., they all heard the quiet voice. "Come and catch me," it said.

"It's in here!" the police officer in the living room shouted. "It's coming from the bookcase!"

Alfred and the two police officers looked at the bookcase. At first, they saw only books. Then they spotted a plastic children's watch on a low shelf in the bookcase. It was a Spider-Man watch, and in a quiet voice, it repeated a line from the movie *Spider-Man*: "Come and catch me." It repeated the line five times. Then it was silent. Alfred picked up the watch and looked at it. The alarm on the watch was set for 2 a.m.

"This is my grandson's watch," Alfred explained to the police officers. "He loved the movie *Spider-Man*, so my daughter bought him this watch a few months ago. I guess he left it here."

The next day, Alfred returned the watch to his grandson. "My Spider-Man watch!" his grandson said. "I was looking for that!"

That night Alfred slept well. The voice was gone.

2 VOCABULARY

Complete the sentences with the words below.

ghost searched spotted widower

1. Nobody could see the person with the quiet voice. Maybe it was a ______.
2. Alfred's wife died a few years ago. He is a ______.
3. Alfred looked everywhere. He ______ every room in his apartment.
4. Alfred and the police officers looked at the bookcase, but didn't see anything unusual. Then they ______ the watch on a low shelf.

3 COMPREHENSION

UNDERSTANDING A SUMMARY

A **Complete the sentences. Write the answers on the lines.**

1. When Alfred's _daughter_ heard the recording, she called the _police_.
2. Every _night_ at 2 a.m., Alfred Mansbridge heard a _quiet_ voice.
3. In a bookcase in the _living_ room, Alfred and the police officers found a children's _watch_.
4. The quiet voice was _gone_ after Alfred returned the watch to his _grandson_.
5. Alfred wanted to record the voice, so he went to a store and _bought_ a _tape_ recorder.

B **Copy the sentences above in the correct order to make a summary of the story. Write your summary on the lines below. The first sentence is done for you.**

2 _Every night at 2 a.m., Alfred Mansbridge heard a quiet voice._

5. ______

1. ______

3 ______

4 ______

______

______

______

UNDERSTANDING QUOTATIONS

Who said it? Match the sentences and the people. Write the letter of the answer on the line.

_c_ 1. "Come and catch me."
_d_ 2. "I *am* tired."
_e_ 3. "I think you're alone too much."
_a_ 4. "It's coming from the bookcase!"
_b_ 5. "I was looking for that!"

a. a police officer
b. Alfred's grandson
c. the quiet voice
d. Alfred
e. Alfred's daughter

REMEMBERING DETAILS

A **Which sentences describe Alfred Mansbridge? Check (✓) six answers. The first one is done for you.**

- [x] 1. He is 69 years old.
- [x] 2. He is a widower.
- [ ] 3. He lives in a big house.
- [x] 4. He lives alone.
- [x] 5. He has a daughter.
- [x] 6. He had trouble sleeping.
- [ ] 7. He is a police officer.
- [x] 8. He is a grandfather.

B **Which sentences describe the quiet voice? Check (✓) six answers.**

- [x] 1. It sounded like a ghost or a child.
- [ ] 2. Alfred heard it only in the kitchen.
- [x] 3. Alfred heard it every night for 15 seconds.
- [x] 4. It said, "Come and catch me."
- [x] 5. It repeated the sentence five times.
- [ ] 6. Alfred's neighbors heard it, too.
- [x] 7. It woke Alfred up.
- [x] 8. It came from a watch.

4 DISCUSSION / WRITING

Alfred had trouble sleeping. Some nights he didn't sleep at all.

A **How many hours do you sleep at night? Line up at the front of the room. The person who sleeps the fewest hours will stand at the beginning of the line. The person who sleeps the most hours will stand at the end of the line. The people in between will stand in order of the number of hours they sleep.**

B **What can you do to get a good night's sleep? Write your ideas on the lines below. For example:**

Don't watch a scary movie before you go to bed.

____

____

____

____

C **Share your ideas with the class.**

UNIT 7

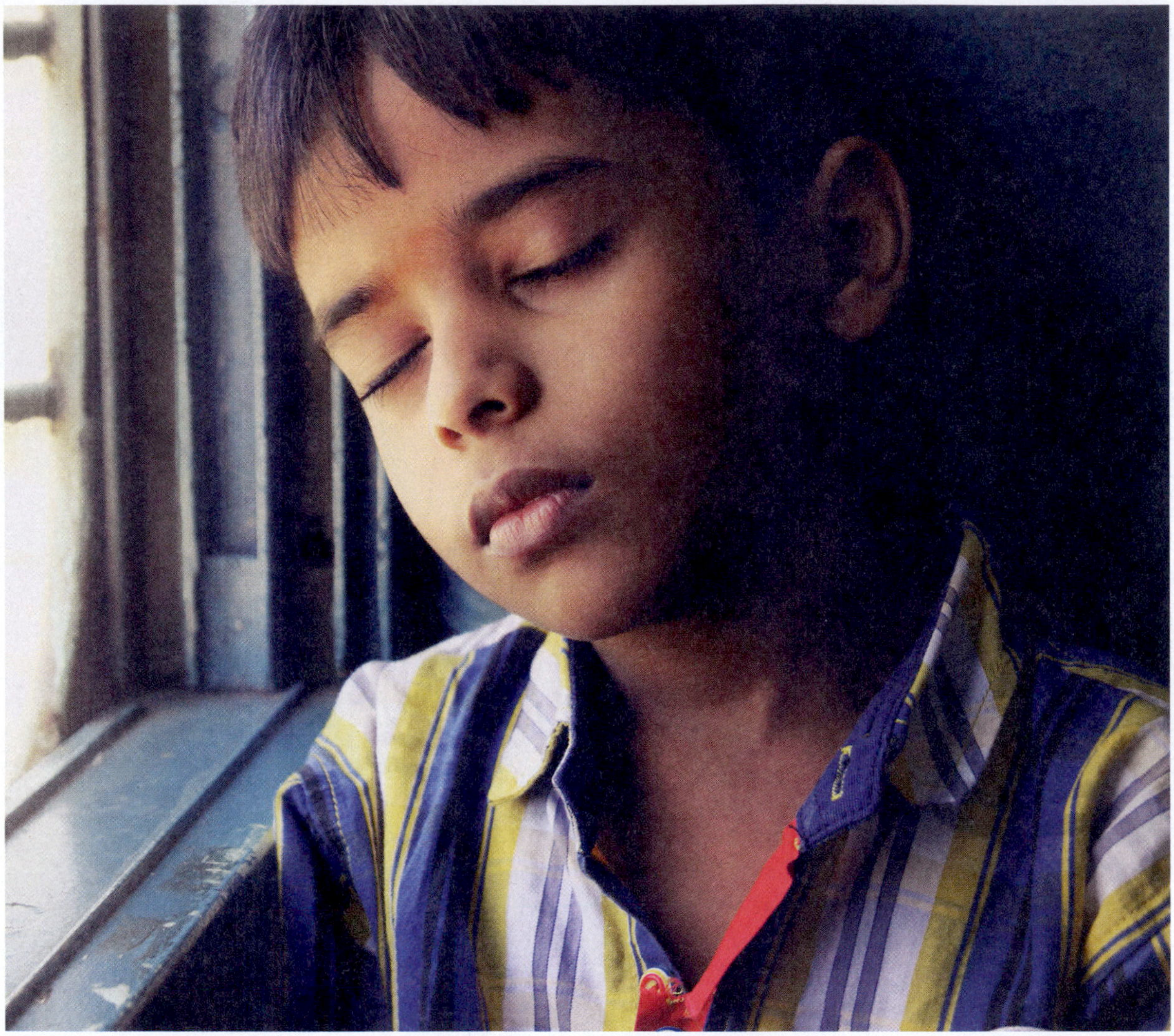

1 PRE-READING

A **Look at the picture. Answer the questions.**

1. What is the boy doing? Where is he?
2. How old is the boy? Where is he from?

B **Read the title of the story. Look at the picture again. Answer the questions.**

1. What do you think this story is about?
2. Can you guess what happens?

The Way Home

Late one night, a little boy, only five years old, got on a train alone. That train ride changed his life forever.

The little boy's name was Saroo. Saroo was living with his mother, brothers, and sister in India. His family was very poor. Every day Saroo and his brother Guddu went to the local train station and got on a train. They looked for money under the seats. Sometimes they found only one or two coins, but every coin helped.

Late one night, Saroo and Guddu were waiting for a train. Saroo was very tired. Guddu pointed to a bench at the station. "Wait for me here," he told Saroo. "I'll come back later." Saroo lay down on the bench and fell asleep. When he woke up, Guddu was gone.

"Guddu! Guddu!" Saroo yelled. But Guddu didn't answer. A train was at the station. "Maybe Guddu is on that train," Saroo thought. He got on the train to look for his brother. Then the train left the station. Saroo tried to open the door to the train's next car, but the door was locked. He lay down and fell asleep.

Fourteen hours later, the train arrived at its final stop, and Saroo got off. He was in Kolkata, a city 1,600 kilometers from his home.

For three weeks, Saroo lived on the streets of Kolkata. "What's your name?" people asked him. "Where are you from?" But nobody could help Saroo because he didn't know his last name or the name of his city. Finally, someone took Saroo to a home for children with no parents. A family in Australia adopted him, and Saroo flew to his new home in Australia.

Saroo grew up happy and healthy in Australia. But he didn't forget his mother in India. When he was 24 years old, he decided to look for her.

For six years, Saroo sat at his computer in his free time and looked at aerial photos of earth. He could look down on every city in India. Which one was his city?

One night Saroo was looking at aerial photos of cities near train tracks when he saw a water tower. Saroo remembered a water tower in his city. Saroo zoomed in on the photo. He could see a bridge, buildings, and streets—and they looked familiar. It was Saroo's city! Now the city had a name: Khandwa.

Saroo flew to India, traveled to Khandwa, and walked to his old house. No one was there. The door was locked, and the house was vacant.

"They moved," a neighbor said. "I'll take you to them."

Saroo's mother was sitting in front of her house when she heard a neighbor screaming, "Your Saroo is back!" She walked down the street and saw a small group of people. In the middle of the group was a handsome young man. He ran to her, and she ran to him. They hugged for a long time. Saroo's mother took her son's hand. Then she took him home.

2 VOCABULARY

Complete the sentences with the words below.

adopted aerial familiar vacant zoomed in

1. A couple in Australia took Saroo as their own child, and he grew up with them. They ____________________ him when he was five.
2. Saroo looked at photos of earth. The photos were taken from an airplane or satellite. They were ____________________ photos.
3. Saroo saw a water tower in a photo. He wanted a better look at the water tower, so he ____________________ on the photo.

4. Saroo remembered a bridge near his house in Khandwa. When he saw the bridge in the photo, it looked ________________ to him.
5. Saroo found his old house in Khandwa, but no people and no furniture were inside. The house was ________________.

3 COMPREHENSION

UNDERSTANDING PLACE

The story happens in three places: Khandwa, India; Kolkata, India; and Australia.

Read each sentence. Where did it happen? Write the number of the place on the line.

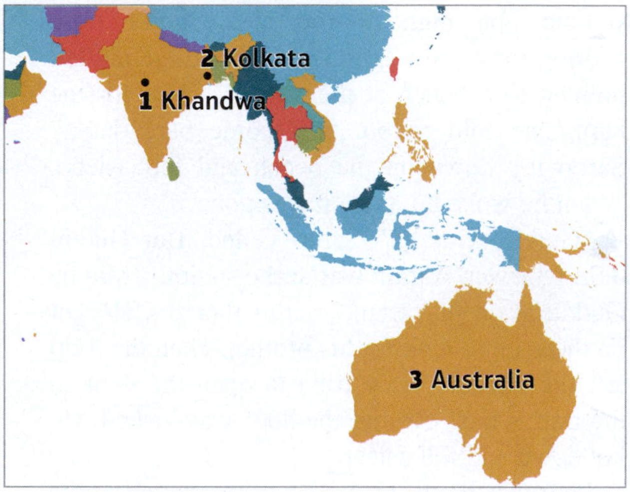

__1__ A neighbor took Saroo to his mother.

____ Saroo grew up happy and healthy.

____ Saroo and his brother looked for money under train seats.

____ Saroo lived on the streets.

____ Saroo got on a train to look for his brother.

____ Saroo looked at aerial photos of earth.

____ Saroo walked to his old house.

____ Someone took Saroo to a home for children with no parents.

FINDING MORE INFORMATION

Read each sentence on the left. Which sentence on the right gives you more information? Write the letter of the answer on the line.

__c__ 1. Saroo and his brother looked for money on trains.

____ 2. Saroo tried to open the door to the train's next car.

____ 3. Saroo saw his city.

____ 4. No one was at Saroo's old house.

____ 5. Saroo's mother saw a small group of people.

a. "They moved," a neighbor told him.

b. A handsome young man was with them.

c. Sometimes they found only one or two coins.

d. Its name was Khandwa.

e. It was locked.

LOOKING FOR INFORMATION

Read each question. Find the answer in the paragraphs on the next page and circle it. Write the number of the question above the answer.

1. Why did Saroo get on the train?
2. How many hours did Saroo ride the train?

3. Where was the train's final stop?
4. How far is Kolkata from Saroo's home?
5. How long did Saroo live on the streets of Kolkata?
6. What two questions did people ask Saroo?
7. Why couldn't people help Saroo?
8. Where did the family who adopted Saroo live?

1

Saroo got on a train to look for his brother. Fourteen hours later, the train arrived at its final stop, and Saroo got off. He was in Kolkata, a city 1,600 kilometers from his home.

For three weeks, Saroo lived on the streets of Kolkata. "What's your name?" people asked him. "Where are you from?" But nobody could help Saroo because he didn't know his last name or the name of his city. Finally, someone took Saroo to a home for children with no parents. A family in Australia adopted him.

4 WRITING / DISCUSSION

A **Imagine this: You are looking at an aerial photo of your native town or city. You can see your home and the area around it. On your own paper, draw what you see when you look down on your home.**

B **On the lines below, write 3–6 sentences about your drawing. Here is what one student wrote.**

My house is in a small town. There is an old school on the next block. The school is vacant now, but boys still play basketball in the playground. A river goes through my town. A street near my house goes to the river. When I was a child, the river was clean, but now it is polluted.

____

____

____

____

____

____

C **Show your drawing to a partner. Tell your partner about your home and the area around it.**

UNIT 8

The rescue of Jessica McClure

1 PRE-READING

A **Look at the picture. Answer the questions.**

1. The little girl in the photo is Jessica McClure. How old do you think she is?
2. What does she have around her body?
3. Who is holding her?

B **Read the title of the story. Look at the picture again. Answer the questions.**

1. What do you think this story is about?
2. Can you guess what happened?

Everybody's Baby

At a day care center in Texas, children were playing outside. One of the children was Jessica McClure. She was 18 months old. Jessica's mother, who worked at the day care center, was watching the children. Suddenly Jessica fell and disappeared. Jessica's mother screamed and ran to her.

A well was in the yard of the day care center. The well was only eight inches across, and a rock always covered it. But children had moved the rock. When Jessica fell, she fell right into the well.

Jessica's mother reached inside the well, but she couldn't feel Jessica. She ran to a phone and called 911 for help.

Men from the fire department arrived. They discovered that Jessica was about 20 feet (six meters) down in the well. For the next hour the men talked and planned Jessica's rescue. Then they told Jessica's parents their plan.

"We can't go down into the well," they said. "It's too narrow. So, we're going to drill a hole next to the well. We'll drill down about 20 feet. Then we'll drill a tunnel across to Jessica. When we reach her, we'll bring her through the tunnel. Then we'll bring her up through our hole."

The men began to drill the hole on a Wednesday morning. "We'll reach Jessica in a few hours," they thought. The men were wrong. They had to drill through solid rock. Two days later, on Friday morning, they were still drilling. And Jessica McClure was still in the well.

During her days in the well, Jessica sometimes called for her mother. Sometimes she slept, sometimes she cried, and sometimes she sang.

All over the world, people waited for news of Jessica. They read about her in newspapers and watched her rescue on TV. Everyone worried about the little girl in the well.

At 8 p.m. on Friday, the men finally reached Jessica and brought her up from the well. Then paramedics rushed her to the hospital. Jessica was dirty, hungry, thirsty, and tired. Her foot and forehead were badly injured. But Jessica was alive. A doctor at the hospital said, "Jessica is lucky she's very young. She's not going to remember this very well."

Today Jessica McClure is a happy, healthy woman in her 30s. She is married and has two children. The doctor who said, "She's not going to remember this very well" was right: Jessica doesn't remember the 58 hours she was in the well. Although Jessica doesn't remember her days in the well, her rescuers and many other people around the world will not forget them. For three days in 1987, Jessica McClure was everybody's baby.

2 VOCABULARY

Complete the sentences with the words below.

day care center   drill   injured   narrow   rushed

1. Jessica's mother took care of small children. She worked at a day care center.
2. The well was only eight inches across. It was ____________________.
3. The men used machines to ____________________ a hole next to the well.
4. Paramedics ____________________ Jessica to the hospital. The ambulance arrived there in minutes.
5. Doctors looked at Jessica's foot and forehead, which were badly ____________________.

3 COMPREHENSION

UNDERSTANDING THE MAIN IDEAS

Circle the letter of the best answer.

1. This story is about
   a. day care centers in Texas.
   b. the rescue of a little girl.
   c. drilling wells.
2. The story has a happy ending because
   a. Jessica was not injured.
   b. Jessica was in the well only two days.
   c. the men rescued Jessica.

UNDERSTANDING TIME RELATIONSHIPS

Find the best way to complete each sentence. Write the letter of the answer on the line.

1. When Jessica fell, __d__
2. When Jessica's mother reached inside the well, _____
3. When the men from the fire department arrived, _____
4. When Jessica was in the well, _____
5. When the rescuers reached Jessica, _____

a. she slept, cried, and sang.
b. they brought her through the tunnel and then up through their hole.
c. she couldn't feel Jessica.
d. she fell right into the well.
e. they discovered that Jessica was about 20 feet down in the well.

REMEMBERING DETAILS

One word in each sentence is not correct. Find the word and cross it out. Write the correct word.

1. Jessica McClure was 18 ~~years~~ months old.
2. A well was in the kitchen of the day care center.
3. When Jessica fell, she fell right into the water.
4. Jessica's mother ran to a phone and wrote 911.
5. The men said, "We're going to drill a cover next to the well."
6. The men had to drill through soft rock.
7. At 8 p.m. on Friday, men reached Jessica and brought her down from the well.
8. Then doctors rushed her to the hospital.

9. A doctor at the hospital said, "Jessica is lucky she's very old."

10. Jessica doesn't remember the 58 days she was in the well.

4 DISCUSSION

The doctor said, "Jessica is lucky she's very young. She's not going to remember this very well."

A Think back to the time when you were very young. Is there an experience you remember? Draw a picture of it in the space below.

B Show your drawing to a small group of classmates. Tell the people in your group about your experience.

5 WRITING

A Read this story. It is in the present tense.

Jessica is playing at a day care center. Suddenly she falls into a well. She falls about 20 feet and can't get out of the well.

Men from the fire department come. They can't go down into the well because it is too narrow. The men decide to drill a hole next to the well.

For the next 58 hours the men drill the hole. Their job is very difficult because they are drilling through solid rock. Finally they reach Jessica and bring her up from the well. Jessica's foot and forehead are badly injured, but she is alive. Everyone is very happy.

B On your own paper, write the story again in the past tense.

Jessica was playing at a day care center. Suddenly she . . .

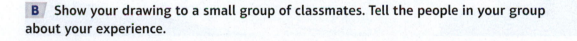

UNIT 9

1 PRE-READING

A **Look at the picture. Answer the question.**

Imagine this: You are very rich. You have more money than you need. What will you do with the extra money? Write some ideas on the lines below. Then share your ideas with the class.

____

____

____

B **Read the title of the story. Look at the picture again. Answer the questions.**

1. What do you think this story is about?
2. Can you guess what happens?

Pay It Forward

In 1971 when Larry Stewart was 22 years old, he lost his job. For weeks he drove from city to city and looked for work. He found nothing. In a small town in Mississippi, his car ran out of gas and he ran out of money. He couldn't pay for a hotel room, so he slept in his car. He had no money to buy food, so he got really hungry. For two days, he ate nothing at all.

Early in the morning, Larry went to a small restaurant. Only one man was working there; he was the restaurant's owner. Larry ate a big breakfast. When the owner gave him the bill, Larry reached into his back pocket. "Oh, no!" he said. "I lost my wallet!" Of course that wasn't true; Larry's wallet was in his car, but there was no money in it.

The owner bent down and reached under Larry's table. When he stood up, he had a $20 bill in his hand. "I think you dropped this," he said. He put the money in Larry's hand. "Yes, I think I did," Larry said. He paid for his breakfast, then pushed his car to a gas station and filled the tank.

Larry decided to drive to Kansas City, Missouri, because he had a cousin there. "Maybe my cousin can help me find work," Larry thought. On the way to Kansas City, Larry thought about the restaurant owner. "He didn't really find that $20 under my table," Larry decided. "He gave me his money."

In Kansas City, Larry found a job. Later he started a cable TV business, and it was a success. Nine years after he arrived in Kansas City, Larry was a rich man.

One day Larry went to a restaurant in Kansas City and ordered a hamburger for lunch. The waitress who took his order looked tired. Larry thought back to 1971, when he was tired, hungry, and out of work. He thought about the small restaurant in Mississippi and the man who had given him $20. When the waitress brought the bill, Larry gave her $20. "Keep the change," he told her. The waitress started to cry. "Thank you, sir," she said. "Thank you very much."

When Larry left the restaurant, he went to his bank and got some $100 bills. All day he walked around Kansas City with the money. When he saw people who looked sad or poor, he gave them a $100 bill. At the end of the day, he felt wonderful.

Larry had a new hobby: giving money away. Sometimes he gave $100 bills to people on the street. Sometimes he went to fast-food restaurants or laundromats and gave money to people there. He returned to the restaurant in Mississippi and gave the owner an envelope with $10,000 in it. When the man opened the envelope, he tried to hand it back. "No, sir," Larry told him. "I came to pay you back." Altogether, Larry gave away more than one million dollars.

"We are here on earth to help one another," Larry said. "Help the people who helped you. Help others, too. Don't just pay it back. Pay it forward."

2 VOCABULARY

Complete the sentences with the words below.

change order ran out of success tank

1. Larry ___ran out of___ money, so he couldn't pay for food or a hotel room.
2. He pushed his car to a gas station and filled the ____________ with gas.
3. Larry's cable TV business made him a rich man. It was a ____________.
4. "I'll have a hamburger," Larry told the waitress who took his ____________.
5. Larry gave the waitress $20 for his hamburger. She didn't give him any money back because he told her, "Keep the ____________."

3 COMPREHENSION

REVIEWING THE STORY

Write the missing words. Then read the story again and check your answers.

When Larry Stewart was a young man, he lost his ___job___ (1.) and couldn't find work. A restaurant ___________ (2.) gave him $20. Larry used the money to buy breakfast and gas. Then he ___________ (3.) to Kansas City, Missouri. He started a cable TV ___________ (4.) there and became a rich man.

After Larry became rich, he began giving ___________ (5.) away. He gave $100 ___________ (6.) to people on the street. He also gave money to people in ___________ (7.) restaurants and laundromats. Altogether, he gave away ___________ (8.) than one million dollars. "Don't just pay it back," Larry said. "Pay it ___________ (9.), too."

UNDERSTANDING CAUSE AND EFFECT

Find the best way to complete each sentence. Write the letter of the answer on the line.

1. Larry lost his job, so ___b___
2. He couldn't pay for a hotel room, so _____
3. He had no money to pay for breakfast, so _____
4. The restaurant owner wanted to help Larry, so _____
5. Larry wanted to help people who looked sad or poor, so _____

a. he told the restaurant owner, "Oh, no! I lost my wallet!"

b. he drove from city to city and looked for work.

c. he gave them $100 bills.

d. he gave him $20.

e. he slept in his car.

FINDING INFORMATION

Read each question. Find the answer in the paragraphs on the next page and circle it. Write the number of the question above the answer.

1. In what year did Larry lose his job?
2. How old was he?
3. How long did he look for work?
4. Where did his car run out of gas?
5. Why did he sleep in his car?
6. For how many days did he eat nothing?
7. When did he go to a small restaurant?
8. How many men were working there?

9. What did Larry eat?
10. What did he say when the owner gave him the bill?

In 1971, when Larry Stewart was 22 years old, he lost his job. For weeks he drove from city to city and looked for work. He found nothing. In a small town in Mississippi, his car ran out of gas and he ran out of money. He couldn't pay for a hotel room, so he slept in his car. He had no money to buy food, so he got really hungry. For two days, he ate nothing at all.

Early in the morning, Larry went to a small restaurant. Only one man was working there; he was the restaurant's owner. Larry ate a big breakfast. When the owner gave him the bill, Larry reached into his back pocket. "I lost my wallet!" he said.

4 DISCUSSION / WRITING

Larry said, "Help the people who helped you." Who is someone who helped you?

A **Fill in the chart below. Write the name of someone who helped you (in a big way or in a small way). In a sentence or two, explain how he or she helped you. Then share your writing with a partner.**

NAME	HOW HE/SHE HELPED ME

B **On your own paper, write a thank-you letter to the person who helped you. Here is what one student wrote.**

Dear Maria,

Thank you for telling me about the English class. I go every Monday, Wednesday, and Friday, and my English is improving.

Antonia

UNIT 10

1 PRE-READING

A Look at the picture. Answer the questions.

1. What spice is this?
2. How do people use it? Why do they use it?

B Read the title of the story. Look at the picture again. Answer the question.

What do you think this story is about?

Please Pass the Bird Brains

Do you have a headache? Eat some bird brains for dinner, and your headache will go away. Do you want beautiful skin? Put some ground pearls into your soup. Your skin will be beautiful. Is your hair turning gray? Eat black rice every day, and you won't have gray hair.

"Eat bird brains, pearls, and black rice?" some people ask. "How strange!" But in traditional Chinese medicine, bird brains, pearls, and black rice are not strange things to eat; they are good things to eat. They are good medicines, too.

There is a saying in Chinese: *yi shi tong yuan*. It means: *Let food be your medicine*. Not all Chinese believe that eating bird brains stops headaches, that soup with ground pearls is good for the skin, or that black rice stops hair from turning gray. But many Chinese do believe that food can be medicine.

Some people don't believe that food can be good medicine. They want to buy their medicine in drugstores, not in supermarkets. Other people want to try medicinal food. They say, "Maybe medicinal food can't help me. But it can't hurt me, either."

How can people try Chinese medicinal food? They can go to China! In China, there are special restaurants that serve it. The menus at these restaurants have a list of dishes. Next to each dish, there is information about the food. The information helps people order. "Queen's Secret," for example, is one dish. Meat from a chicken with black skin is one of the ingredients. It is for women who want to look young. A dish called "Spring Fountain" is made with lamb and ginseng. It helps control blood sugar. There is even a dish for people whose marriages are unhappy. It is called "Lover's Soup."

Outside of China, it is difficult to find restaurants that serve medicinal food. But it is not difficult to find stores that sell Chinese herbs and spices. A market near Los Angeles sells dried herbs in color-coded bags. The colors tell people how the herbs can help them. Herbs in purple bags, for example, give people energy.

Of course the market sells ginger. Ginger is a common spice in Chinese cooking. It gives food a nice flavor. The Chinese believe that ginger is medicinal. It is good for stomach problems and for colds and infections. The market sells fresh ginger root, ginger paste in a tube, and ginger powder in a bag or in a jar.

When people buy ginger at the market, what are they buying? Are they buying a spice? Are they buying medicine? Or are they buying both?

2 VOCABULARY

Complete the sentences with the words below.

common	dried	ground	ingredients	strange

1. For beautiful skin, some people eat very, very small pieces of pearls. They put ____ground____ pearls in their soup.
2. Some people think that eating bird brains is unusual and surprising. But in traditional Chinese medicine, it is not ____________________.
3. There are many things in the dish "Queen's Secret." Chicken is one of the ____________________.
4. People who like to keep herbs for a long time don't buy fresh herbs. They buy ____________________ herbs.
5. The Chinese use ginger often. It is a ____________________ spice in Chinese cooking.

3 COMPREHENSION

UNDERSTANDING THE MAIN IDEAS

Circle the letter of the best answer.

1. "Please Pass the Bird Brains" is about
   a. eating bird brains.
   b. Chinese medicinal food.
   c. delicious food and spices.
2. If people want to try Chinese medicinal dishes,
   a. they can go to restaurants in Los Angeles.
   b. they can travel to China.
   c. they can buy them in supermarkets.
3. The menus at restaurants that serve medicinal food
   a. are color-coded.
   b. have only three dishes.
   c. tell how the dishes can help people.

REMEMBERING DETAILS

Read the list of medicinal foods on the left. Match each food with the reason people eat it. Write the letter of the answer on the line.

c 1. bird brains	a. for stomach problems and colds
____ 2. soup with ground pearls	b. to look young
____ 3. black rice	c. to stop headaches
____ 4. ginger	d. to stop hair from turning gray
____ 5. chicken with black skin	e. to control blood sugar
____ 6. a dish with lamb and ginseng	f. for beautiful skin

FINDING MORE INFORMATION

Read each sentence on the left. Which sentence on the right gives you more information? Write the letter of the answer on the line.

d 1. There is a saying in Chinese.	a. Next to each dish, there is medicinal information about the dish.
____ 2. The menus at some restaurants in China have a list of dishes.	b. People can buy it fresh, in a paste, or in a powder.
____ 3. A market near Los Angeles sells dried herbs.	c. They are in color-coded bags.
____ 4. The Los Angeles market sells ginger.	d. It translates as: *Let food be your medicine.*

4 DISCUSSION / WRITING

Not only the Chinese use medicinal food. People all over the world use medicinal food and home remedies.

A **Find out if your classmates use medicinal food and home remedies. Ask a classmate, "Do you know any home remedies for these problems?"**

- a cold
- an earache
- a headache
- hiccups
- a stomachache
- a backache
- a sore throat
- a burn
- an insect bite

B **Write about three or four home remedies in your country or family for different health problems. For example:**

When someone has an earache, people in Italy put a little warm olive oil in the ear. Putting olive oil in the ear is a home remedy for an earache.

UNIT 11

Margaret Patrick and Ruth Eisenberg

1 PRE-READING

A Look at the picture. Answer the questions.

1. The women in the photo are Margaret Patrick and Ruth Eisenberg. What is unusual about the way they are playing the piano?
2. Why do you think they are playing that way?

B Read the title of the story. Look at the picture again. Answer the questions.

1. Do you think the women are old friends or new friends?
2. What do you think this story is about?
3. Can you guess what happens?

Margaret Patrick… Meet Ruth Eisenberg

Ruth Eisenberg and Margaret Patrick played the piano together for several years. They gave concerts in the United States and in Canada, and they were often on TV. They were famous.

Why were they famous? They played the piano well, but they were not famous because they played well. They were famous because Mrs. Eisenberg played the piano with only her right hand, and Mrs. Patrick played the piano with only her left hand. They sat next to each other and played the piano together. Mrs. Eisenberg played one part of the music, and Mrs. Patrick played the other part.

Mrs. Eisenberg and Mrs. Patrick didn't always play the piano with only one hand. When they were younger, they played with two hands. Mrs. Patrick was a piano teacher. She taught hundreds of students. She taught her own children, too. Then, when she was 69 years old, Mrs. Patrick had a stroke. She couldn't move or speak. Gradually she got better, but her right side was still very weak. She couldn't play the piano anymore. She was very sad.

Playing the piano was Mrs. Eisenberg's hobby. She often played five or six hours a day. Then, when she was 80 years old, she, too, had a stroke. She couldn't move the left side of her body, so she couldn't play the piano anymore. She was very sad.

A few months after her stroke, Mrs. Eisenberg went to a senior citizens' center. There were a lot of activities at the center, and Mrs. Eisenberg wanted to keep busy. Mrs. Patrick wanted to keep busy, too. A few weeks later, she went to the same center. The director was showing her around the center when Mrs. Patrick saw a piano. She looked sadly at the piano. "Is anything wrong?" the director asked. "No," Mrs. Patrick answered. "The piano brings back memories. Before my stroke, I played the piano." The director looked at Mrs. Patrick's weak right hand and said, "Wait here. I'll be right back." A few minutes later, the director came back with Mrs. Eisenberg. "Margaret Patrick," the director said, "meet Ruth Eisenberg. Before her stroke, she played the piano, too. She has a good right hand, and you have a good left hand. I think you two can do something wonderful together."

"Do you know Chopin's Waltz in D Flat?" Mrs. Eisenberg asked Mrs. Patrick. "Yes," Mrs. Patrick answered. The two women sat down at the piano and began to play. Mrs. Eisenberg used only her right hand, and Mrs. Patrick used only her left hand. The music sounded good. The women discovered that they loved the same music. Together they began to play the music they loved. They were not sad anymore.

Mrs. Patrick said, "Sometimes God closes a door and then opens a window. I lost my music, but I found Ruth. Now I have my music again. I have my friend Ruth, too."

2 VOCABULARY

Which words have the same meaning as the words in *italics*? Write the letter of the answer on the line.

b 1. Mrs. Patrick got better. It happened *gradually*.

____ 2. Her right side was *weak*.

____ 3. Mrs. Eisenberg enjoyed playing the piano. It was *her hobby*.

____ 4. Mrs. Patrick and Mrs. Eisenberg were both *senior citizens*.

____ 5. There were a lot of *activities* at the senior center.

a. more than 65 years old

b. slowly

c. things to do

d. not strong

e. something she did in her free time

3 COMPREHENSION

UNDERSTANDING CONNECTIONS

Find the best way to complete each sentence. Write the letter of the answer on the line.

1. Mrs. Eisenberg played the piano with her right hand, and b
2. Mrs. Eisenberg played one part of the music, and _____
3. Mrs. Patrick was a piano teacher, and _____
4. Mrs. Patrick was 69 years old when she had a stroke, and _____
5. Mrs. Patrick said that sometimes God closes a door, and _____
6. Mrs. Patrick had her music back, and _____

a. Mrs. Eisenberg played the piano as a hobby.
b. Mrs. Patrick played with her left hand.
c. then God opens a window.
d. Mrs. Patrick played the other part.
e. she had a new friend, too.
f. Mrs. Eisenberg was 80.

MAKING INFERENCES

Find the best way to complete each sentence. Write the letter of the answer on the line. (The answers are not in the story; you have to guess.)

1. Mrs. Eisenberg and Mrs. Patrick gave concerts in the United States and in Canada, so probably b
2. Mrs. Patrick taught the piano to hundreds of students, so probably _____
3. Mrs. Patrick and Mrs. Eisenberg went to the same senior citizens' center, so probably _____
4. Both women knew Chopin's Waltz in D Flat, so probably _____

a. they lived in the same city.
b. they traveled often.
c. they liked classical music.
d. she was a piano teacher for many years.

UNDERSTANDING A SUMMARY

Imagine this: You want to tell the story "Margaret Patrick...Meet Ruth Eisenberg" to a friend. You want to tell the story quickly, in only six sentences. Which six sentences tell the story best? Check (✓) your answer.

☐ 1. Two women played the piano. One woman was a piano teacher; she taught hundreds of students and her own children, too. The other woman played the piano as a hobby; she often played five or six hours a day. Both women had a stroke and couldn't play the piano anymore. They were very sad. The women wanted to keep busy, so they went to a senior citizens' center.

☐ 2. Two women had a stroke and couldn't play the piano anymore. One woman couldn't use her left arm, and the other woman couldn't use her right arm. One day the women met at a senior citizens' center. They discovered they could play the piano together. They began to give concerts. One woman played one part of the music with her left hand, and the other woman played the other part with her right hand.

4 DISCUSSION / WRITING

Mrs. Patrick and Mrs. Eisenberg had a lot in common: They both played the piano, they loved the same music, and they both had a stroke.

A **Talk with a partner to find out what you have in common. You will need to ask each other questions—for example, "Are you a good dancer?" or "When is your birthday?"**

B **On the lines below, make a list of three things you and your partner have in common. Do not write about things you can see (for example, your height or the color of your eyes). Here is what one student wrote.**

YOU
ME
We both have two brothers but no sisters.
We both like to play soccer.
Our birthdays are in June.

YOU
ME

C **Share your list with the class.**

UNIT 12

1 PRE-READING

A Look at the picture. Answer the questions.

1. Why is money sometimes in plastic bags?
2. What happened to this bag? How much money do you think is in it?

B Read the title of the story. Look at the picture again. Answer the questions.

1. What does the expression *finders keepers* mean?
2. What do you think this story is about?
3. Can you guess what happens?

Finders Keepers?

Mel Kiser was driving along a busy highway in Columbus, Ohio. He saw an armored truck a few cars ahead of him. Suddenly the back doors of the armored truck opened, and a blue plastic bag fell out of the truck. A car in front of Mr. Kiser hit the bag. The bag ripped, and money spilled out. Then another bag fell out of the truck, and another. Money was flying everywhere.

At first, drivers thought the green papers on the highway were leaves. Then they realized that the green papers were not leaves—they were money! Drivers slammed on their brakes and stopped right in the middle of the highway. People jumped out of their cars and began picking up money. They were putting 10-, 20-, and 100-dollar bills into their pockets. One man was yelling, "Money, money, money! It's all free! Grab some while you can!"

Mr. Kiser also got out of his car. He grabbed a plastic bag of money, put the bag in his car, and drove away.

Later Mr. Kiser counted the money. He had $57,000. For the next two hours, Mr. Kiser thought about the money. He dreamed about spending it. He needed a new furnace for his house. He wanted to take a vacation in Florida. But he decided to return the money. He drove to the police station and gave the police the $57,000.

Mr. Kiser returned $57,000, and other people returned money, too. But over one million dollars was still missing. The armored truck company offered a 10 percent reward. "If you return $1,000, for example, we will pay you $100," the company said. Mel Kiser had returned $57,000, so the company gave him a reward of $5,700. A few more people returned money and got rewards, but most of the money—almost a million dollars—was still missing.

Then the armored truck company got some help. A man telephoned and said, "I was driving along the highway when I saw a traffic jam ahead," the man said. "I didn't want to be in the traffic jam, so I took the next exit and got off the highway. Then I saw the money. People were running everywhere. I had a camera in my car, and I took some pictures. Would you like the pictures?"

"Yes!" answered the armored truck company. The company gave the pictures to the police. The police looked closely at the pictures. They looked at the cars, the license plates, and the people's faces. They tried to find the people who had taken the money, but they didn't have much luck.

One man who had taken money telephoned a Columbus newspaper. The man did not give his name. "I took two bags of money," he said. "I'm going to take the money and leave Columbus. I have enough money for the rest of my life."

2 VOCABULARY

Complete the sentences with the words below.

armored truck | grabbed | ripped | slammed on their brakes

1. The truck ahead of Mel Kiser was small and strong, and it carried money. It was an __armored truck__.
2. When cars hit the plastic bags, the bags broke and opened. The bags ________.
3. When the drivers saw money flying everywhere, they stopped suddenly. They ________.
4. People jumped out of their cars to pick money up off the street. They ________ 10-, 20-, and 100-dollar bills.

3 COMPREHENSION

REMEMBERING DETAILS

One word in each sentence is not correct. Find the word and cross it out. Write the correct word.

1. Mel Kiser was driving along a ~~quiet~~ busy highway in Columbus, Ohio.
2. He saw an armored bus a few cars ahead of him.
3. Suddenly the back doors of the armored truck closed.
4. A blue paper bag fell out of the truck.
5. The bag ripped, and leaves spilled out.
6. People jumped out of their houses and began picking up money.
7. They were putting 10-, 30-, and 100-dollar bills into their pockets.
8. The armored truck company offered a 10 percent tax.
9. More people returned money, but almost a million pennies were still missing.

UNDERSTANDING TIME RELATIONSHIPS

Find the best way to complete each sentence. Write the letter of the answer on the line.

1. When the back doors of the armored truck opened, c
2. When cars hit the plastic bags, _____
3. When drivers realized that the green papers were money, _____
4. When Mr. Kiser went to the police station, _____
5. When the armored truck company offered a reward, _____

a. they slammed on their brakes.
b. the bags ripped.
c. blue plastic bags fell out of the truck.
d. more people returned money.
e. he returned $57,000.

MAKING INFERENCES

Find the best way to complete each sentence. Write the letter of the answer on the line. (The answers are not in the story; you have to guess.)

1. There is a busy highway in Columbus, Ohio, so probably b
2. The driver of the armored truck didn't stop, so probably _____
3. Mel Kiser needed a furnace, so probably _____
4. Mel Kiser returned all the money, so probably _____
5. One man said, "I have enough money for the rest of my life," so probably _____

a. he didn't realize that money was falling from the truck.
b. Columbus is a big city.
c. he found a lot of money.
d. he is an honest man.
e. the weather is sometimes cold in Ohio.

4 DISCUSSION

The man in the story found a bag with $57,000 in it. He decided to give the money to the police.

A **Imagine this: You are walking in a big city in your native country. You find a bag on the sidewalk. There is $57,000 in the bag. What will you do with the money? Check (✓) one answer.**

- ☐ I will keep the money.
- ☐ I will give the money to the police. I will tell the police, "Try to find the owner of the money."
- ☐ I will try to find the owner of the money myself.
- ☐ I will give the money to poor people.
- ☐ ______________________________

(Write your own answer.)

B **Explain your answer in a small group.**

5 WRITING

Imagine that you see bags of money on a highway. What will you do? Complete the story.

Last week I was driving along a busy highway when I saw an armored truck a few cars ahead of me. Suddenly the back doors of the truck opened, and a blue plastic bag fell out of the truck. A car in front of me hit the bag. The bag ripped, and money spilled out. Then another bag fell out of the truck, and another. Money was flying everywhere. I . . .

____

____

____

____

____

____

____

____

____

____

____

UNIT 13

1 PRE-READING

A **Look at the picture. Answer the questions.**

1. The things in the photo are for sale at a flea market. What kinds of things can people buy at flea markets?
2. Are there flea markets in your native country? If so, do you sometimes shop there? What kinds of things do you buy?

B **Read the title of the story. Look at the picture again. Answer the questions.**

1. What do you think this story is about?
2. Can you guess what happens?

The Husband

Sharon Clark will never forget the day she met Giovanni Vigliotto. She was working in Indiana, as the manager of a large flea market. Early one morning, he walked into her office. "I'd like to rent some space at the flea market," he said. "I have a lot of used things to sell. Do you have any space?"

"Yes, I do," she answered.

When the flea market closed at the end of the day, Giovanni invited Sharon to have dinner with him. She was 43 years old, divorced, and a little lonely. She said yes.

For the next four months, Sharon saw Giovanni often. He was not a handsome man—he was short and heavy, and he had a big nose. But he was intelligent, polite, and kind. She fell in love with him. "Marry me," Giovanni said.

Sharon thought it over. Her mind told her, "Don't do it. You don't know him well enough." But her heart told her, "Do it. Take a chance." Sharon listened to her heart and married Giovanni.

After they got married, Giovanni said he wanted to move to Canada. "I have a beautiful house there," he said. "Let's sell your house and move to Canada." Sharon sold her house and made a profit of $55,000. She wanted to take her furniture to Canada, so she and Giovanni rented a truck. "I'll drive the truck, and you can drive your car," he said. "You'd better give me the $55,000. It's dangerous for a woman to travel with that much money."

"You're right," Sharon agreed, and she gave Giovanni the $55,000.

On the way from Indiana to Canada, Giovanni told Sharon he had to stop in Ohio on business. "You go on ahead," he told her. They decided to meet at a hotel in Canada.

Giovanni never arrived at the hotel. At first Sharon was worried. "Maybe Giovanni was in an accident," she thought. She called the police in Ohio. "No," the police said, "Giovanni Vigliotto wasn't in an accident here." So where was Giovanni? He was gone, and so were her furniture and her money.

Sharon was angry. She wanted her money and her furniture back. She wanted to find Giovanni. "I met him at a flea market," she thought. "Maybe he's at a flea market somewhere."

For months Sharon went to flea markets all over the United States. At a flea market in Florida, she found Giovanni. He was selling used furniture. Some of it was hers. Sharon called the police.

When the police arrested Giovanni, Sharon's story was in newspapers and on TV. A woman in New Jersey called the police. "Giovanni is my husband, too!" she said. Then another woman called the police, and another, and another. "Giovanni is my husband!" the women said. All the women told similar stories: They met Giovanni at a flea market; they sold their houses; he took their furniture and their money. Altogether, 105 women were married to Giovanni.

A judge sentenced Giovanni to 34 years in prison. "I want you to stay in prison for a long time," the judge told Giovanni. "I want to be sure there will be no wife number 106."

2 VOCABULARY

Which words have the same meaning as the words in *italics*? Write the letter of the answer on the line.

e 1. Giovanni said, "*I'd like* to rent some space."

_____ 2. "*You'd better* give me the $55,000," Giovanni told Sharon.

_____ 3. Sharon said, "*I agree*."

_____ 4. Sharon looked for Giovanni *all over* the United States.

_____ 5. The police *arrested Giovanni*.

_____ 6. All the women's stories were *similar*.

a. took him to prison
b. You should
c. almost the same
d. everywhere in
e. I want
f. You're right

3 COMPREHENSION

REMEMBERING DETAILS

Read the summary of the story "The Husband." There are 11 mistakes in the summary. Find the mistakes and cross them out. Write the correct words. The first one is done for you.

Sharon Clark was the ~~owner~~ manager of a large fruit market. Giovanni rented space at the market because he had some new things to sell. At the end of the day, he invited Sharon to have dessert with him.

For the next four weeks, Sharon saw Giovanni often, and she fell in love with him. She didn't know him well, but she listened to her mind and married him.

Giovanni said he wanted to move to Mexico because he had a house there. So Sharon sold her house and made a profit of $5,000. She and Giovanni rented a car, and he drove away with her furniture and her money. He never arrived in Canada.

Sharon found Giovanni at a flea market in California and called the police. After the police arrested Giovanni, many women told similar stories about him. Altogether, he had 55 wives.

FINDING MORE INFORMATION

Read each sentence on the left. Which sentence on the right gives you more information? Write the letter of the answer on the line.

__c__ 1. Giovanni was not a handsome man.

_____ 2. Giovanni wanted to move to Canada.

_____ 3. Giovanni was selling used furniture.

_____ 4. All of the women told similar stories.

a. He said he had a beautiful house there.

b. They met Giovanni at a flea market; they sold their houses; he took their furniture and their money.

c. He was short and heavy, and he had a big nose.

d. Some of it was Sharon's.

UNDERSTANDING TIME AND PLACE

Read the phrases from the story. Which phrases tell you *when* something happened? Write them in the *WHEN* column. Which phrases tell you *where* something happened? Write them in the *WHERE* column.

- early one morning
- at the flea market
- at the end of the day
- for the next four months
- after they got married
- on the way from Indiana to Canada
- at the hotel
- all over the United States

WHEN	WHERE
early one morning	

4 DISCUSSION

Sharon knew Giovanni for four months. Then she married him. But her mind told her, "Don't do it. You don't know him well enough."

A **How long should you know someone before you get married? Write your answer on the line.**

____

B **Explain your answer in a small group. (If you are married, tell the class how long you knew your husband or wife before you got married.)**

5 WRITING

Sharon met Giovanni at a flea market. When the flea market closed at the end of the day, Giovanni invited Sharon to have dinner with him.

Interview a classmate, friend, or relative who is married. Ask, "How did you meet your husband (or wife)?" Write the story on your own paper. Here is what one student wrote.

Every Sunday morning, my mother and her family went for a walk near the seaside. What they didn't know was that a young sailor was looking at them from a ship with his binoculars. My father fell in love with my mother. One Sunday he introduced himself to her. That happened 52 years ago, and they have been happily married for 50 years.

UNIT 14

1 PRE-READING

A Look at the picture. Answer the questions.

1. What animal is this? Is it a pet?
2. Where can someone sell this animal?

B Read the title of the story. Look at the picture again. Answer the questions.

1. What is an auction?
2. Can you guess what happens?

The Auction

Katie Fisher was excited. It was July 15—the day of the animal auction. "Today I'm going to sell my lamb," she thought.

Seventeen-year-old Katie lived on a farm in Madison County, Ohio. Every July there was an animal auction in Madison County. Children from farms all over the county brought their best animals to an arena. They sold their animals to the farmer who paid the highest price. "I hope I get a good price for my lamb," Katie thought.

On the afternoon of the auction, Katie walked into the center of the arena with her lamb. People were a little surprised when they saw Katie. She had no hair. She had no hair because of chemotherapy. Katie had cancer. The chemotherapy had stopped the cancer, and Katie felt much better. But Katie's parents had a lot of medical bills to pay. Katie wanted to sell her lamb and pay some of her medical bills.

The auctioneer decided to say a few words about Katie. "This young lady needs money for her medical bills," the auctioneer said. "Let's give her a good price for her lamb." Then the auctioneer began the auction.

"Who'll give me one dollar a pound for this lamb?" he began.

"One dollar!" a farmer said.

"I hear one dollar," the auctioneer said. "Who'll give me two dollars a pound?"

"Two dollars!" another farmer said.

"I hear two dollars," the auctioneer continued. "Who'll give me three dollars?"

The auctioneer continued to raise the price of the lamb, and the farmers continued to offer more money. Finally, Katie's lamb sold for twelve dollars a pound.

Katie was happy. Lambs usually sold for two dollars a pound, but her lamb sold for twelve dollars a pound! She took her lamb to the farmer who bought it. The farmer paid Katie for the lamb and then said something surprising: "Keep the lamb," he told Katie. "Sell it again."

Katie walked back into the center of the arena with her lamb. Smiling, the auctioneer said, "Well, I guess I have to sell this lamb again." A second farmer bought the lamb, this time for eight dollars a pound.

When the auctioneer sold the lamb for the second time, something amazing happened. The farm families in the arena began chanting, "Sell it again! Sell it again!" When Katie took her lamb to the second farmer, he paid her for the lamb. Then he smiled and said, "You heard the people. Keep the lamb. Sell it again."

Katie walked back into the center of the arena with her lamb, and the crowd cheered. The auctioneer sold Katie's lamb again…and again …and again. Every time the auctioneer sold the lamb, the crowd chanted, "Sell it again! Sell it again!"

That afternoon the farmers of Madison County, Ohio, bought Katie's lamb 36 times. All 36 farmers paid Katie, but not one farmer took the lamb. Katie went home with enough money to pay all her medical bills. She also went home with her lamb.

2 VOCABULARY

Complete the sentences with the words below.

auctioneer	chanted	cheered	crowd	offer

1. Hundreds of farm families went to the animal auction. There was a big ____crowd____ of people.
2. Before he began the auction, the ________________ said a few words about Katie.

3. The farm families repeated the same words. "Sell it again! Sell it again!" they ________________.

4. Every time the price of the lamb went up, a farmer said, "I'll pay that." The farmers continued to ____________________ Katie more and more money.

5. The people at the auction were happy when Katie walked back into the center of the arena with her lamb, so they ____________________.

3 COMPREHENSION

REMEMBERING DETAILS

One word in each sentence is not correct. Find the word and cross it out. Write the correct word.

1. Katie Fisher was excited because she was going to sell her ~~cow.~~ lamb
2. Seven-year-old Katie lived on a farm in Madison County, Ohio.
3. Every December there was an animal auction in Madison County.
4. Children from farms all over the world brought their best animals to an arena.
5. They sold their animals to the farmer who paid the lowest price.
6. Lambs usually sold for two cents a pound, but Katie's lamb sold for twelve dollars a pound.
7. Katie took her lamb to the auctioneer who bought it.
8. The farmer thanked Katie for the lamb and then said, "Keep the lamb."

UNDERSTANDING CAUSE AND EFFECT

Find the best way to complete each sentence. Write the letter of the answer on the line.

1. Katie wanted to sell her lamb __e__
2. The people in the arena were surprised when they saw Katie _____
3. The second farmer who bought the lamb told Katie, "You heard the people" _____
4. Katie got a lot of money for her lamb _____
5. Katie went home with her lamb _____

a. because the farm families were chanting, "Sell it again."
b. because the farmers bought it again and again.
c. because the farmers who bought the lamb didn't take it.
d. because she had no hair.
e. because she needed money for medical bills.

UNDERSTANDING A SUMMARY

Imagine this: You want to tell the story "The Auction" to a friend. You want to tell the story quickly, in only four sentences. Which four sentences tell the story best? Check (✓) your answer.

☐ **1.** A seventeen-year-old girl who had cancer needed money for her medical bills. She decided to sell her lamb at an auction in Madison County, Ohio. The auction happens every July in Madison County. Farm children take their best animals to an arena and sell them to the farmer who pays the highest price.

☐ **2.** A seventeen-year-old girl who had cancer needed money for her medical bills. She decided to sell her lamb at an auction. Every time she sold her lamb, the farmer who bought it didn't take it. She sold the lamb 36 times and went home with enough money to pay all her medical bills.

4 DISCUSSION

The farm families did something kind for Katie. People do kind things every day. For example: They give money to poor people; they help people who are lost; they open doors for people who are carrying packages.

Did someone do something kind for you? Did *you* do something kind for someone? In a small group, tell your classmates about it.

5 WRITING

Katie Fisher keeps a diary. Every night, she writes down what happened that day. What did Katie write on the night of July 15? Finish the page in Katie's diary.

July 15

This afternoon I went to the arena to sell my lamb. I walked into the center of the arena. The auctioneer told the people I needed money for medical bills. Then he began the auction.

The lamb sold for twelve dollars a pound! I took my lamb to the farmer who bought it. He . . .

____

____

____

____

____

____

____

____

UNIT 15

1 PRE-READING

A **Look at the picture. Answer the questions.**

1. What things do people put in washing machines by mistake?
2. How can you dry money that you put in a washing machine?

B **Read the title of the story. Look at the picture again. Answer the questions.**

1. What do you think this story is about?
2. Can you guess what happens?

Money to Burn

Lillian Beard whistled and smiled while she worked. "Why are you so happy?" her co-workers asked her.

"Last week I got my income tax refund," Lillian answered. "This morning I went to the bank and cashed the check. I have $462 in my pocket. I'm thinking about the money. How will I spend it?"

After work Lillian came home and decided to wash some clothes. She looked at the jeans she was wearing. They were dirty, so she put them in the washing machine, too. Ten minutes later, she remembered: "The money! It's still in the pocket of my jeans!" Lillian ran to the washing machine and took out the jeans. The money was still in the pocket, but it was wet. Lillian put the money on the kitchen table to dry.

A few hours later, the money was still wet. "Hmm," Lillian thought. "How can I dry this money?" Then Lillian had an idea. She could dry the money in her microwave oven! Lillian put the money in the microwave, set the timer for five minutes, and left the kitchen.

When Lillian came back a few minutes later, she saw a fire in the microwave. She opened the oven door, blew out the fire, and looked at her money. The money was burned.

The next day, Lillian took the burned money to the bank. A teller at the bank told her, "If I can see the numbers on the burned bills, I can give you new money." Unfortunately, the teller found numbers on only a few bills. The teller took those bills and gave Lillian $17.

A newspaper reporter heard about the burned money. He wrote a story about Lillian for the newspaper. Several people read the story and called the newspaper. "Tell Ms. Beard to send the burned money to the U.S. Department of Treasury," the people said. "Maybe she can get her money back."

Every year about 30,000 people send damaged money to the Treasury Department. Experts there look carefully at the damaged money. Sometimes they can give people new money for the damaged money. Once a farmer dropped his wallet in a field, and a cow ate his money—thousands of dollars. The farmer killed the cow and sent the cow's stomach, with the money inside, to the Treasury Department. The experts gave the farmer new money.

Lillian sent her money to the Treasury Department. The experts looked at Lillian's burned money and sent her a check for $231.

What did Lillian buy with the money? She didn't buy anything. She gave the $231 to friends who needed money. Lillian said, "When I burned the $462, I thought, 'Well, my money is gone.' The check for $231 was a big surprise. I decided to give the money to my friends. Money is important, but people are more important to me."

2 VOCABULARY

Complete the sentences with the words below.

experts	income	refund	set the timer	teller

1. Lillian works and earns money. She pays tax on the money she earns. She pays ___income___ tax.
2. When Lillian paid her income tax, she gave the government too much money. The government gave her some money back. Lillian got a ______________ on her income tax.

3. Lillian wanted the microwave oven to dry the money, so she ____________________ for five minutes.

4. People at the Treasury Department know a lot about money. They are ____________________.

5. Lillian took her burned money to the bank and showed it to someone who worked there. The ____________________ took some of the bills and gave Lillian $17.

3 COMPREHENSION

REMEMBERING DETAILS

What did Lillian Beard do with her money? Check (✓) seven answers. The first one is done for you.

- [x] 1. She put it in her pocket.
- [ ] 2. She washed it with her jeans.
- [ ] 3. She put it on the kitchen table to dry.
- [ ] 4. She counted it many times.
- [ ] 5. She burned it in her microwave oven.
- [ ] 6. She showed it to a teller at the bank.
- [ ] 7. She sent it to the Treasury Department.
- [ ] 8. She spent it.
- [ ] 9. She gave it to friends.

UNDERSTANDING PRONOUNS

Look at the pronouns. (They are in *italics*.) What do they mean? Write the letter of the answer on the line.

__b__ 1. Lillian cashed *it*.

_____ 2. Lillian decided to wash *them*.

_____ 3. *It* was damaged.

_____ 4. Lillian set *it* for five minutes.

_____ 5. *He* wrote a story about Lillian.

_____ 6. *It* ate a farmer's money.

_____ 7. *They* looked carefully at Lillian's burned money.

_____ 8. Lillian gave *them* money.

a. experts at the Treasury Department
b. her income tax refund check
c. her jeans
d. the timer
e. a newspaper reporter
f. a cow
g. her friends
h. Lillian's money

UNDERSTANDING A SUMMARY

Imagine this: You want to tell the story "Money to Burn" to a friend. You want to tell the story quickly, in only four sentences. Which four sentences tell the story best? Check (✓) your answer.

☐ 1. A woman who got a $462 income tax refund went to the bank and cashed the check. At work she was very happy because she had $462 in her pocket. After work she went home and washed her jeans. She forgot to take the money out of the pocket, so the money got wet.

☐ 2. When a woman washed her jeans, she forgot that she had $462 in the pocket. She tried to dry the wet money in her microwave oven, but burned it. She sent the burned money to experts at the U.S. Treasury Department, who mailed the woman a check for $231. The woman gave the money to her friends.

4 DISCUSSION

Lillian Beard lived in the United States, in the state of Indiana. In Indiana, people pay tax on income, houses and land, the food they eat in restaurants, the things they buy in stores, and tickets for movies and sporting events.

A **On the lines below, make a list of things that are taxed in your native country. Then ask a partner what is taxed in his or her native country. Write your partner's list on the lines.**

MY COUNTRY	MY PARTNER'S COUNTRY
______________________	______________________
______________________	______________________
______________________	______________________
______________________	______________________

B **Tell the class what you learned about taxes in your partner's native country.**

5 WRITING

Look at a coin or bill. Then describe the money in a paragraph on your own paper. Here is what one student wrote.

I have a five-dinar bill from Bahrain. It is worth about 13 American dollars. Its colors are blue and green. On one side of the bill, the language is Arabic. On the other side of the bill, the language is English. If you hold the bill up to the light, you can see a drawing of an ox's head.

UNIT 16

The stamp to honor the Mendez family

1 PRE-READING

A **Look at the picture. Answer the questions.**

1. What country is the stamp from?
2. How much does the stamp cost?
3. What names do you see on the stamp?
4. What are the two young people doing?

B **Read the title of the story. Look at the picture again. Answer the questions.**

1. What do you think this story is about?
2. Can you guess what happens?

The School and the Stamp

In October 2007, post offices in the United States began selling a new stamp. On the stamp, there is a drawing of two strong young people with black hair. They are reading a book, and a bright sun is shining on them.

There is a true story behind that stamp. The story begins in 1945 with a man named Gonzalo Mendez.

Gonzalo Mendez was born in Mexico and came to the United States when he was a little boy. He dropped out of school at age ten to become a farm worker. He and his wife, Felicitas, had three children and owned a small but successful café in Santa Ana, California.

In 1945, Gonzalo heard about an asparagus farm that was for rent. The farm was in Westminster, California, about seven miles from Santa Ana. Gonzalo was excited about renting the farm; this was his chance to be a real farmer, not a farm worker. He and Felicitas talked it over, and they decided to move to Westminster.

After the Mendez family moved to Westminster, Felicitas took the three children to an elementary school there. That is when the story behind the stamp really begins. Felicitas found out that her children could not attend the school. They had to attend the "Mexican school."

The "Mexican school" was in an old building. The textbooks were old, too. When the children came home and described the school to their father, he told them, "You will not go to the 'Mexican school.' You will go to the other school."

Gonzalo talked to other Latino parents in Westminster. "The other elementary school is better than the 'Mexican school,'" he told them. "Let's go to court. Let's fight to get our children into that other school."

The Latino parents agreed with Gonzalo: The other elementary school was better in every way. But the "Mexican school" was closer. "Our children will stay at the 'Mexican school,' close to home," the Latino parents told Gonzalo.

So Gonzalo decided to fight alone. He spent all his savings to hire a lawyer, and he went to court.

Latino families in other cities in Southern California heard about Gonzalo Mendez. Their children, too, had to attend "Mexican schools." Four Latino families decided to help Gonzalo. They gave him money for the lawyer and went to court with him.

The judge decided that the Latino families were right: Separate schools for Latino children were unfair. At that time, there were 5,000 Latino children who had to attend "Mexican schools" in Southern California. After the judge's decision, they could attend any school.

The Mendez children went to elementary school and then to high school; some went to college, too.

In 2007, the Mendez family celebrated the new stamp, which they liked very much. They especially liked the way the two young readers bend like plants toward the sun. "That's how it is," they said. "Education brings light into people's lives. This small stamp tells our whole story."

2 VOCABULARY

Which words have the same meaning as the words in *italics*? Write the letter of the answer on the line.

__d__	1. There is a *drawing* of two strong young people on the stamp.	a. stopped going to
_____	2. Gonzalo *dropped out of* school when he was ten.	b. an opportunity
_____	3. The Mendez children *attended* the "Mexican school."	c. were students at
_____	4. Gonzalo had *a chance* to become a real farmer.	d. picture

3 COMPREHENSION

UNDERSTANDING THE MAIN IDEAS

Complete the sentences. Write your answers on the lines.

1. When does the story behind the stamp begin?

   It begins in ____1945____ with a man named Gonzalo ____________.

2. Why was Gonzalo excited about renting the asparagus farm?

   It was his chance to be a real ____________, not a ____________ ____________.

3. What did Felicitas do after the Mendez family moved to Westminster?

   She took her ____________ to an ____________ school there.

4. Where was the "Mexican school"?

   It was in an ____________ building.

5. What did Gonzalo Mendez tell the Latino parents in Westminster?

   He said, "Let's ____________ to get our children into that other ____________."

6. Why did the Latino families in Westminster want their children to stay at the "Mexican school"?

   It was ____________ to home.

7. How did the four Latino families help Gonzalo?

   They gave him money for the ____________ and went to ____________ with him.

8. What did the judge decide?

   The judge decided that ____________ schools for Latino children were ____________.

UNDERSTANDING PRONOUNS

Look at the pronouns. (They are in *italics*.) What do they mean? Write the letter of the answer on the line.

__a__ 1. *They* began selling a new stamp in October 2007.

____ 2. A bright sun is shining on *them*.

____ 3. *They* had to go to "Mexican schools."

____ 4. *They* were old.

____ 5. Gonzalo talked to *them*.

a. post offices in the United States

b. the textbooks at the "Mexican school"

c. Latino children in Southern California

d. the young people on the stamp

e. Latino parents in Westminster

FINDING INFORMATION

Read each question. Find the answer in the paragraph below and circle it. Write the number of the question above the answer.

1. Where was Gonzalo Mendez born?
2. When did he come to the United States?
3. How old was he when he dropped out of school?
4. Why did he drop out of school?
5. What was his wife's name?
6. How many children did they have?
7. What did they own?
8. Where was it?

Gonzalo Mendez was born in Mexico and came to the United States when he was a little boy. He dropped out of school at age ten to become a farm worker. He and his wife, Felicitas, had three children and owned a small but successful café in Santa Ana, California.

4 DISCUSSION / WRITING

The judge decided that separate schools for Latino children were unfair. The postage stamp about the decision has a drawing of two strong young people. They are reading a book, and a bright sun is shining on them.

A **Design a postage stamp. In the space below, draw a picture of an important person, place, or thing in your community. Then complete the sentences below the picture.**

This is ____. He/She/It is important because ____
____.

B **Share your picture and your sentences with a partner.**

UNIT 17

Costa Rican fishermen after their rescue

1 PRE-READING

A **Look at the picture. Answer the questions.**

1. How do you think the men feel?
2. What do you see in the water?

B **Read the title of the story. Look at the picture again and the map. Answer the questions.**

1. What do you think this story is about?
2. Can you guess what happens?

A Long Fishing Trip

On a warm January morning, Joel Gonzalez kissed his wife goodbye. Joel is a fisherman, and he was going on a short fishing trip. "I'll see you in a week," he said. But Joel did not see his wife in a week. He did not see his wife again for a long, long time.

Joel left his house and went to the harbor in Puntarenas, Costa Rica. He got on a fishing boat. Four other fishermen were on the boat, too. The boat left the harbor, and the men began to fish.

The first few hours on the ocean were not unusual. Then there was a terrible storm. The storm lasted for 22 days. When the storm finally stopped, the men checked their boat. Their fishing nets were gone. The engine and the radio didn't work. There was no food, and there was no fresh water.

For the next few hours, the men talked and planned. "How can we survive on the ocean?" they asked one another. Without their nets, the men couldn't fish. But they could reach out of the boat and catch big turtles. The men didn't want to eat raw turtle meat, so they needed a fire for cooking. They tore down the boat's wood cabin and made a fire with the wood.

They needed protection from the sun and rain, so they built a simple roof. The roof held rainwater, too. The men could drink rainwater from the roof.

For the next five months, the men ate turtles—when they caught them. They drank rainwater—when it rained. Often there was no food and no water, and the men were hungry and thirsty. Sometimes they thought, "We are going to die soon."

Joel wrote a letter to his wife. "My dear Edith," Joel wrote. "If I die, I hope someone will send you this letter. Then you will know how I died. I had the best in life—a great woman and beautiful children. I love you, Edith. I love you."

In June it didn't rain for a long time, and the men ran out of water. They were thin and weak, and they thought, "We are going to die now." They lay down and closed their eyes. After a while, it began to rain. The men stood up and licked the water from the roof. Then all five men began to cry.

Ten days later, on June 15, a Japanese fishing boat found the men. They were 4,000 miles (6,437 kilometers) from Costa Rica.

Nobody sent Joel's letter to his wife. He showed it to his wife himself. Joel will always keep the letter. The letter, he says, helps him remember. "On the ocean, I realized that I love my wife and children very, very much. My family is everything to me. I don't want to forget that."

2 VOCABULARY

Complete the sentences with the words below.

harbor	nets	ran out of	raw	survive

1. Joel went to the ___harbor___ in Puntarenas. There were many boats there.
2. The fishermen needed their ______________ to catch fish.
3. The men didn't want to eat ______________ turtle meat, so they built a fire to cook the meat.
4. The men didn't want to die on the ocean; they wanted to ______________.
5. The men had nothing to drink because they ______________ water.

3 COMPREHENSION

UNDERSTANDING THE MAIN IDEAS

There are two correct ways to complete each sentence. Circle the letters of the *two* correct answers.

1. Joel Gonzalez
   a. is a fisherman.
   b. is single.
   c. lives in Puntarenas, Costa Rica.
2. After the storm,
   a. there was a hole in the boat.
   b. the boat's engine and radio didn't work.
   c. there was no food or fresh water on the boat.
3. To survive, the men
   a. ate turtle meat.
   b. drank rainwater.
   c. caught birds.
4. In June the men thought they were going to die because they
   a. had no more water.
   b. were all very sick.
   c. were thin and weak.
5. When the Japanese fishing boat found the men,
   a. they were 4,000 miles from Costa Rica.
   b. it was five months after the storm.
   c. only three of the fishermen were alive.
6. Joel wrote a letter that
   a. he will always keep.
   b. he showed to his wife.
   c. somebody sent to his wife.

UNDERSTANDING REASONS

Find the best way to complete each sentence. Write the letter of the answer on the line.

1. The men left Puntarenas b
2. The men reached out of their boat _____
3. The men tore down the boat's cabin _____
4. Joel wrote his wife a letter _____
5. Joel will keep his letter _____

a. to help him remember that his family is everything to him.
b. to fish on the ocean.
c. to tell her how he died.
d. to catch turtles.
e. to make a fire with the wood.

UNDERSTANDING A SUMMARY

Imagine this: You want to tell the story "A Long Fishing Trip" to a friend. You want to tell the story quickly, in only four sentences. Which four sentences tell the story best? Check (✓) your answer.

☐ 1. Joel Gonzalez is a Costa Rican fisherman. One January morning, he kissed his wife goodbye and went on a fishing trip. Joel didn't return for five months. While he was away, he wrote his wife a long letter and told her he loved her very much.

☐ 2. Five Costa Rican fishermen were in a terrible storm that lasted for 22 days. After the storm, they were lost at sea for five months. To survive, they ate turtles and drank rainwater. When a Japanese fishing boat found the men, they were 4,000 miles from Costa Rica.

4 DISCUSSION

The fishermen in the story were lost at sea for months. Fishing is dangerous work.

A **Read the list of dangerous jobs below. Which job do you think is the most dangerous? Discuss this question in a small group. Check (✓) your group's answer.**

☐ construction worker
☐ police officer
☐ pilot
☐ fisherman
☐ farmer
☐ truck driver
☐ cashier in a small store
☐ coal miner

B **Tell the class which job your group chose and why.**

5 WRITING

Joel wrote a letter to his wife. The end of Joel's letter is missing. Complete Joel's letter.

Dear Edith,

If I die, I hope someone will send you this letter. Then you will know how I died. When we left the harbor, everything was fine. Then, a few hours later, there was a terrible storm. It lasted for 22 days. After the storm, we checked our boat. Our fishing nets were . . .

____

____

____

____

____

____

UNIT 18

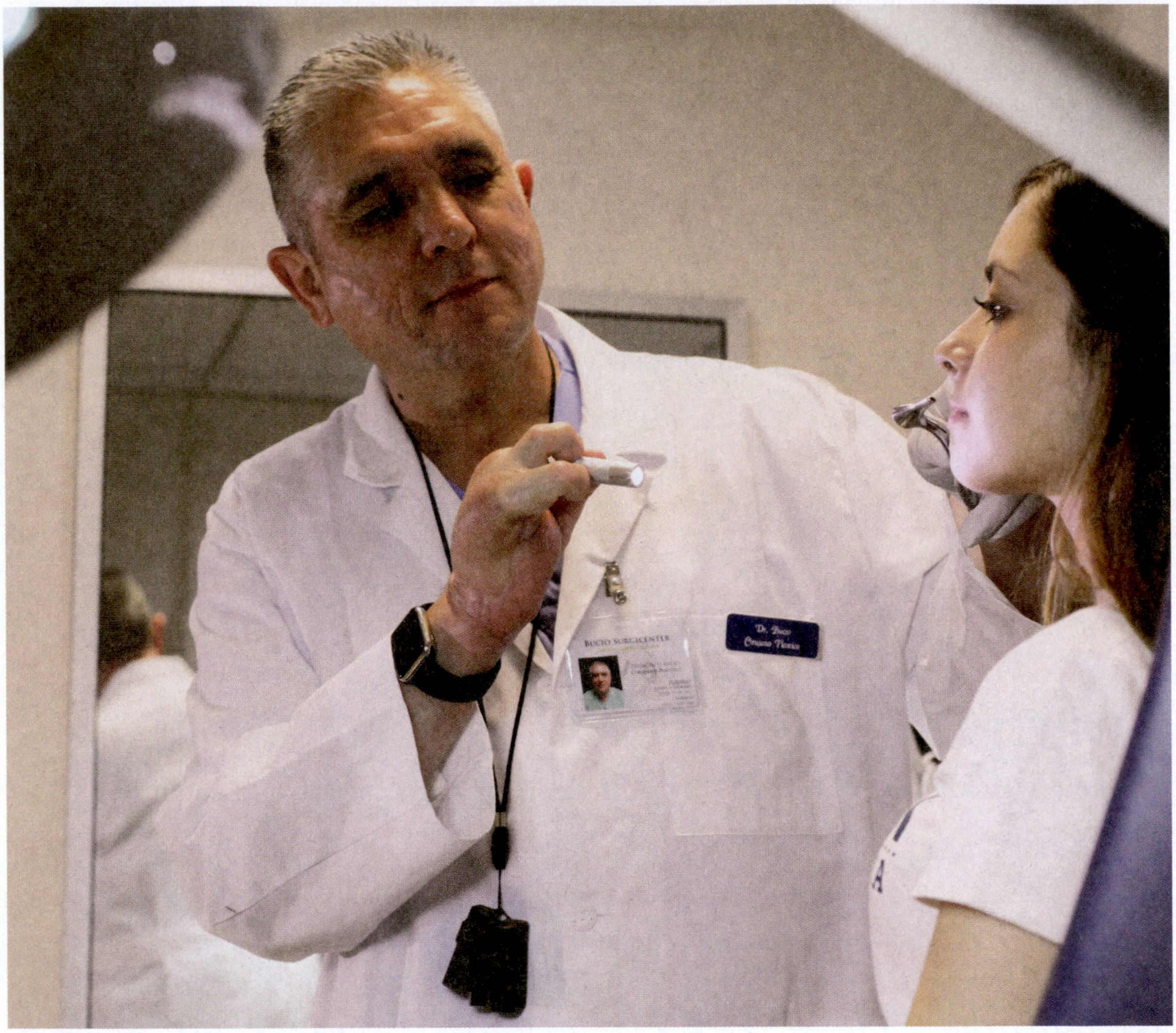

Dr. Francisco Bucio

1 PRE-READING

A **Look at the picture. Answer the questions.**

1. What is this man's work?
2. What is unusual about his right hand?

B **Read the title of the story. Look at the picture again. Answer the questions.**

1. What do you think this story is about?
2. Can you guess what happens?

The Surgeon

On September 19, 1985, Dr. Francisco Bucio was getting dressed for work. His roommate, Angel Alcantara, was combing his hair. Both Francisco and Angel were doctors in Mexico City. They lived and worked together on the fourth floor of General Hospital. Suddenly the hospital began to shake. "Earthquake!" Francisco said. The hospital shook and shook. Then the hospital collapsed. Francisco and Angel fell four floors to the ground below. Three floors of the hospital fell on top of them. The doctors were trapped under a mountain of steel and concrete.

"Angel!" Francisco called to his friend. Angel moaned in pain. Then he was silent. Francisco knew that his friend was dead. Francisco wanted to cry because Angel was dead. But he told himself, "Keep calm." Then he realized that his right hand was hurt. "Oh, no; oh, no!" Francisco cried. "I can't lose my right hand. My right hand is my future."

For the next four days, Francisco was trapped under the hospital. Every twelve hours, Angel's watch beeped at exactly 7:30. "Angel's watch helped me," Francisco said. "I knew what day it was. But I wondered about my family. Were they safe? And I wondered about Mexico City."

On the third day, Francisco became very thirsty. He dreamed of rivers with no water. He dreamed of ships on dry land.

Then, on the fourth day, rescue workers found Francisco. His right hand was trapped under concrete. The rescue workers wanted to cut off Francisco's hand. "No!" said Francisco.

When rescue workers carried Francisco out of the hospital, he still had his hand. But four fingers were badly crushed. Doctors had to cut off all four fingers on Francisco's right hand. Only his thumb remained. During the next months, Francisco had five operations on his hand. His hand looked better, but it didn't work well. Francisco wanted to be a surgeon. But he needed his right hand to operate on patients.

Then Francisco heard about a surgeon in California who was an expert in hand surgery. Six months after the earthquake, the surgeon operated on Francisco. He cut off two of Francisco's toes and sewed the toes on Francisco's hand. The toes became new fingers for Francisco, and the new fingers worked well.

A year later, Francisco returned to the surgeon in California who had operated on him. He didn't go back as a patient; he went back as a student. Francisco wanted to be an expert surgeon, and his doctor was an expert. Francisco studied with his doctor for three months. Then he returned to Mexico and became a plastic surgeon.

"I know how patients feel," Dr. Bucio said. "I can sympathize and understand. I had six operations, and so much pain—too much pain. Sometimes people joke. They say I'm the surgeon who operates with his feet. OK, my hand isn't beautiful, but I like it. It works."

2 VOCABULARY

Which words have the same meaning as the words in *italics*? Circle the letter of the answer.

1. The hospital *collapsed*.
   a. The hospital disappeared.
   (b.) The hospital fell down.
2. The doctors were *trapped* under a mountain of steel and concrete.
   a. A mountain of steel and concrete was on top of the doctors. They couldn't move.
   b. The doctors climbed a mountain of steel and concrete.

3. Angel *moaned* in pain.
   a. Angel made a sound because he was in pain.
   b. Angel closed his eyes because he was in pain.

4. "I know how patients feel," Dr. Bucio said. "I can *sympathize* and understand."
   a. "I understand patients' feelings and pain because I, too, had a lot of pain."
   b. "My patients are kind people, and I like them very much."

3 COMPREHENSION

UNDERSTANDING THE MAIN IDEAS

There are two correct ways to complete each sentence. Circle the letters of the *two* correct answers.

1. On September 19, 1985,
   a. there was an earthquake in Mexico City.
   b. Francisco Bucio was a patient in a hospital.
   c. General Hospital in Mexico City collapsed.
2. During the four days Francisco was trapped under the hospital, he
   a. talked to his friend.
   b. wondered about his family.
   c. became very thirsty.
3. When rescue workers carried Francisco out of the hospital,
   a. he still had both hands.
   b. the fingers on his right hand were badly crushed.
   c. his right leg was broken.
4. The surgeon who was an expert in hand surgery
   a. cut off two of Francisco's toes.
   b. sewed the toes on Francisco's right hand.
   c. worked at General Hospital in Mexico City.
5. Today Francisco Bucio
   a. lives in the United States.
   b. is a plastic surgeon.
   c. knows how his patients feel.

UNDERSTANDING TIME RELATIONSHIPS

Find the best way to complete each sentence. Write the letter of the answer on the line.

1. On September 19, 1985, __e__
2. Every twelve hours, _____
3. On the third day, _____
4. On the fourth day, _____
5. Six months after the earthquake, _____

a. rescue workers found Francisco.
b. an expert in hand surgery operated on Francisco.
c. Francisco became very thirsty.
d. Angel's watch beeped.
e. there was an earthquake in Mexico City.

UNDERSTANDING A SUMMARY

Imagine this: You want to tell the story "The Surgeon" to a friend. You want to tell the story quickly, in only five sentences. Which five sentences tell the story best? Check (✓) your answer.

☐ 1. A hospital in Mexico City collapsed during an earthquake. One of the doctors was trapped under the hospital for four days. He was rescued, but the fingers on his right hand were badly crushed, and doctors had to cut them off. Later, an expert in hand surgery cut off two of the doctor's toes and sewed the toes on the doctor's right hand. The doctor is now a surgeon and operates on patients.

☐ 2. In 1985 there was an earthquake in Mexico City, and a hospital collapsed. A doctor who lived and worked in the hospital fell four floors to the ground below. Three floors of the hospital fell on top of him, and he was trapped under a mountain of steel and concrete. During his four days under the hospital, the doctor worried about his right hand. He also worried about his family and about Mexico City.

4 DISCUSSION / WRITING

On September 19, 1985, there was an earthquake in Mexico. An earthquake is a natural disaster.

A **On the map below, look at the places where natural disasters sometimes happen in the United States. Discuss new vocabulary with your classmates.**

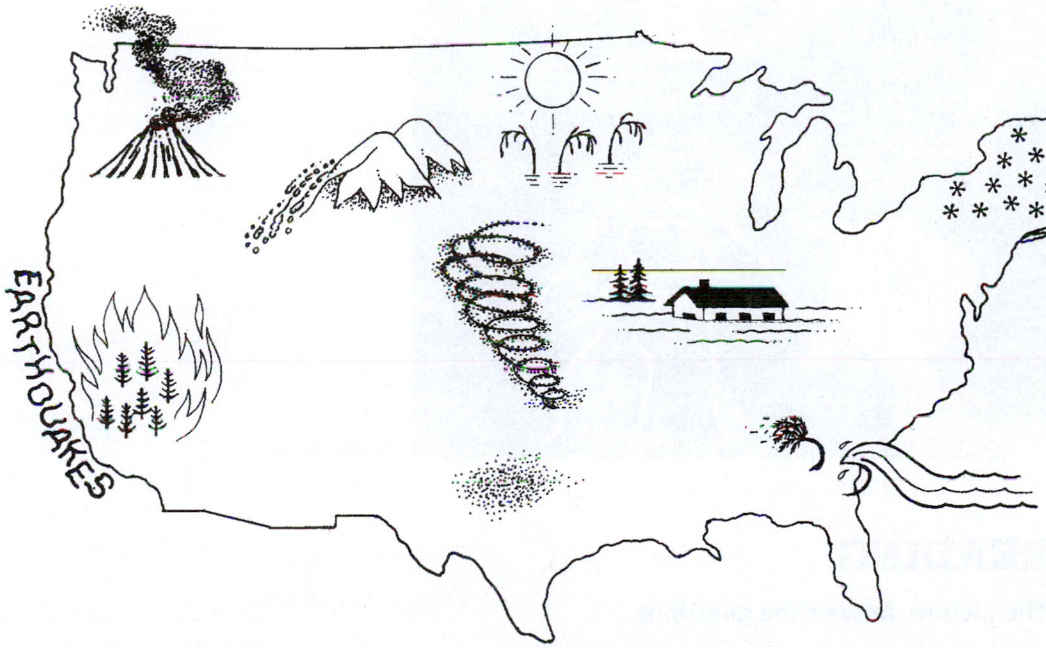

B **On your own paper, draw a map of your native country. Mark the places where natural disasters sometimes happen. Then show your map to a partner. Tell your partner about natural disasters in your native country.**

C **On your own paper, write about a natural disaster that happened in your native country, or write about a natural disaster that *you* experienced.**

UNIT 19

Mona Shaw

1 PRE-READING

A Look at the picture. Answer the questions.

1. How old is the woman?
2. How does she feel?
3. What is she going to do with the hammer?

B Read the title of the story. Look at the picture again. Answer the questions.

1. What do you think this story is about?
2. Can you guess what happens?

Customer Service?

Mona Shaw is a quiet grandmother who lives a quiet life in a quiet suburb of Washington, D.C. But one afternoon Mona made a lot of noise with a hammer. She didn't make noise because she was building something or fixing something. She made a lot of noise because she was angry.

Mona's troubles began when she got a letter from a big telephone company. "Sign up now for our special offer," the letter said. "We'll give you three services—telephone, TV service, and high-speed Internet—for only $100 a month." That seemed like a good deal, so Mona called the company. "I'd like to sign up for your special offer," she said.

"Great!" a company representative said. "A technician will be at your house on Monday."

Mona stayed home all day on Monday. The technician didn't come.

On Wednesday the technician finally came. First, he disconnected Mona's old telephone service. Then he tried to connect the new telephone service. But he had a problem, and he couldn't finish the job. "I'll come back tomorrow," he said.

The technician didn't come back. Now Mona had a problem: She had no telephone service. She was worried. She was 75 years old, and she had a bad heart. "What if I need to call 911 for help?" Mona thought. She went to the company's office.

"May I help you?" a smiling customer service representative asked Mona.

"A technician came to my house and disconnected my old phone service, but he couldn't connect the new service," Mona said. "Can someone come as soon as possible to finish the job?"

"You need to talk to the manager," the customer service representative said. "Please take a seat."

Mona sat down and waited...and waited... and waited...and waited. Two hours later, the customer service representative told her, "I'm really sorry. The manager went home. You'll have to come back another day."

Mona went to a neighbor's house and called the company. "Someone will come to your house next Tuesday," a company representative said.

Mona waited all day Tuesday. Nobody came. At 4:30 that afternoon, Mona went down to the basement, got her husband's hammer, and went back to the company's office. She walked over to the customer service representative's computer. BAM! She hit the computer's monitor with the hammer. BAM! She hit the keyboard. BAM! She hit the telephone that was next to the computer.

"I don't have telephone service," she told the customer service representative. "Now you don't, either." BAM! She hit the phone again.

A few minutes later, the police arrived and arrested Mona. Later, a judge told Mona, "You have to pay $345 for the damage to the computer and the phone." That was okay with Mona. "I don't mind paying the money," she said. "It was worth it. I feel so much better."

Mona has good telephone service now. It is with a different company.

2 VOCABULARY

Complete the sentences with the words below.

damage	don't mind	good deal	technician	What if

1. Telephone, TV, and Internet service can cost $200 a month or more. But one company was giving the three services for only $100 a month. That was a ___good deal___.
2. Mona needed someone to disconnect her old telephone service and connect the new service. The company said, "We'll send a ____________."

3. Mona was thinking about the future. "Maybe I'll have a problem with my heart," she thought. "________________ I need to call 911?"

4. Mona broke a lot of things at the company's office. She had to pay $345 for the ________________.

5. Mona had to pay $345, but that was okay with her. "I ________________ paying the money," she said.

3 COMPREHENSION

UNDERSTANDING THE MAIN IDEAS

Circle the letter of the best answer.

1. This is a story about a woman who
   a. is good at building and fixing things.
   b. had trouble with her computer.
   (c.) got very angry at a company.

2. The woman went to the company's office and
   a. hit things with a hammer.
   b. told the manager, "I'm never coming here again."
   c. talked to a customer service representative for an hour.

3. Now the woman says she feels
   a. sorry for what she did.
   b. much better.
   c. angry at the judge.

REMEMBERING DETAILS

A **Which sentences describe Mona? Check (✓) six answers. The first one is done for you.**

- [x] 1. She is a grandmother.
- [ ] 2. She usually lives a quiet life.
- [ ] 3. She lives in a suburb of Washington, D.C.
- [ ] 4. She works for a telephone company.
- [ ] 5. She is 75 years old.
- [ ] 6. She has trouble walking.
- [ ] 7. She has a bad heart.
- [ ] 8. She has a basement in her house.

B **Why was Mona angry with the telephone company? Check (✓) four answers.**

- ☐ 1. On Monday she waited all day for the technician, but he didn't come.
- ☐ 2. The technician disconnected her old phone service, but he couldn't connect her new service.
- ☐ 3. The company said its special offer cost $100, but it cost $300.
- ☐ 4. Mona waited for two hours to talk to the manager.
- ☐ 5. The company's office was open only two hours a day.
- ☐ 6. A company representative told Mona, "Someone will come to your house next Tuesday," but nobody came.

UNDERSTANDING WORD GROUPS

Read each group of words. One word in each group doesn't belong. Find the word and cross it out.

technician	computer	hammer	police
~~nurse~~	lamp	build	teacher
customer service representative	monitor	fix	arrest
company representative	keyboard	cook	judge

4 DISCUSSION / WRITING

A **In your native country, what do you do if you have a problem with something you bought—if, for example, it is broken or doesn't work? Tell the class.**

B **Have you ever had a bad experience with a company? Tell the class about it.**

C **What can you do if you have a problem with a company? In a small group, make a list of things you can do. On the lines below, write your ideas. Then share them with the class.**

____

____

____

____

____

____

UNIT 20

1 PRE-READING

A **Look at the picture. Answer the questions.**

1. Why do people sometimes tie a letter to a balloon? What do they write in the letter?
2. What happens when someone finds a balloon with a letter?

B **Read the title of the story. Look at the picture again. Answer the questions.**

1. What do you think this story is about?
2. Can you guess what happens?

The Mermaid Balloon

"Grandma!" little Desiree exclaimed. "It's my daddy's birthday. How will I send him a birthday card?"

Desiree's grandmother looked at Desiree and sighed. She didn't know what to say. Desiree's father had died nine months earlier. Desiree didn't understand. She was only four years old.

"I have an idea," her grandmother said. "Let's write your daddy a letter. We can tie the letter to a balloon and send it up to heaven. What should we write?"

Desiree told her grandmother to write, "Happy Birthday, Daddy. I love you and miss you. Please write me on my birthday in January."

Desiree's grandmother wrote Desiree's message and their address on a small piece of paper. Then Desiree, her mother, and her grandmother went to a store to buy a balloon. Desiree looked quickly at the helium-filled balloons and said, "That one! The one with the mermaid!"

They bought the mermaid balloon and tied Desiree's letter to it. Then Desiree let the balloon go. For an hour, they watched the balloon go higher and higher. Finally, it disappeared. "Did you see that?" Desiree exclaimed. "Daddy reached down and took my balloon! Now he's going to write me back!"

Desiree released the balloon in California. The wind caught the balloon and carried it east. Four days later, it came down 3,000 miles away, near a lake in eastern Canada. The name of the lake was Mermaid Lake.

Wade MacKinnon, a Canadian man, was hunting ducks at Mermaid Lake when he found Desiree's balloon and letter. He took them home to his wife. She decided to send Desiree a birthday present. She also wrote her a letter. The letter said:

Dear Desiree,

Happy Birthday from your daddy. I guess you wonder who we are. Well, my husband, Wade, went duck hunting, and guess what he found! A mermaid balloon that you sent your daddy. There are no stores in heaven, so your daddy wanted someone to do his shopping for him. I think he picked us because we live in a town called Mermaid. I know your daddy loves you very much and will always watch over you.

Lots of love,
The MacKinnons

When the package from the MacKinnons arrived, Desiree was not at all surprised. "Daddy remembered my birthday!" she exclaimed.

Desiree's mother wrote the MacKinnons to thank them for the present and the letter. During the next few weeks, she and the MacKinnons telephoned each other often. Then Desiree, her mother, and her grandmother flew to Canada to meet the MacKinnons. The MacKinnons took them to Mermaid Lake and showed them where the balloon had landed.

Now, whenever Desiree wants to talk about her father, she calls the MacKinnons. After she talks to them, she feels better.

People often say, "What a coincidence—the mermaid balloon landed at Mermaid Lake!" Desiree's mother is not sure it was just a coincidence. She says, "I think that somehow my husband picked the MacKinnons. It was his way to send his love to Desiree. She understands now that her father is with her always."

2 VOCABULARY

Which words have the same meaning as the words in *italics*? Circle the letter of the answer.

1. "Grandma!" Desiree *exclaimed*. "It's my daddy's birthday!"
   (a.) said suddenly, with strong feeling　　b. said slowly, with a very quiet voice

2. Desiree's grandmother didn't know what to say. She *sighed*.
   a. cried silently　　b. took in and let out a long breath

3. Desiree *released* the balloon.
   a. opened her eyes and looked at the balloon   b. opened her hand and let the balloon go

4. Wade MacKinnon was *hunting* ducks.
   a. trying to shoot   b. trying to paint

5. Desiree's mother thinks her husband *picked* the MacKinnons to send his love to Desiree.
   a. chose   b. paid

3 COMPREHENSION

UNDERSTANDING THE MAIN IDEAS

Circle the letter of the best answer.

1. What was the coincidence in the story?
   a. Desiree and her father have the same birthday, January 12.
   b. The mermaid balloon came down at Mermaid Lake.
   c. The MacKinnons also have a four-year-old daughter.

2. Desiree feels better now because
   a. she got a lot of presents for her birthday.
   b. she can talk to the MacKinnons about her father.
   c. she spends a lot of time with her grandmother.

REMEMBERING DETAILS

One word in each sentence is not correct. Find the word and cross it out. Write the correct word.

1. Desiree tied a ~~present~~ letter to a helium-filled balloon.

2. The balloon had a picture of a fish on it.

3. Desiree released the balloon in Arizona.

4. The wind carried the balloon south.

5. Four years later, the balloon came down 3,000 miles away.

6. The balloon landed near a mountain in eastern Canada.

7. A Canadian man was feeding ducks when he found Desiree's letter.

8. The MacKinnons decided to send Desiree a birthday cake and a letter.

FINDING MORE INFORMATION

Read each sentence on the left. Which sentence on the right gives you more information? Write the letter of the answer on the line.

b 1. Desiree wrote her father a letter.

____ 2. Desiree chose a balloon at the store.

____ 3. The balloon came down near a lake.

____ 4. A Canadian man found the balloon.

a. It was in eastern Canada, and its name was Mermaid Lake.

b. It said, "Please write me on my birthday in January."

c. It was filled with helium, and it had a picture of a mermaid on it.

d. His name was Wade MacKinnon, and he was hunting ducks.

4 DISCUSSION

The mermaid balloon landed at Mermaid Lake. That was a coincidence. Can you find any coincidences among your classmates?

A **Complete the sentences. (Skip the sentences you can't complete.)**

1. My birthday is ______________ (month) ______________ (day).
2. Once I broke a bone in my ______________.
3. Last summer I took a trip to ______________.
4. A car I like is ______________.
5. I like to play ______________.
6. Last night I dreamed about ______________.

B **In a small group, take turns reading your sentences. Did any students complete a sentence in the same way? Tell the class about any coincidences you discovered.**

5 WRITING

Write a letter on your own paper. Put your letter in a small plastic bag. Tie your letter to a helium-filled balloon and let the balloon go. Here is what one student wrote.

My name is Andrea. I am a student at the American Language Institute in Indiana, PA. If you find my letter, please write me and tell me how far my balloon went. My address is:

American Language Institute
Eicher Hall
Indiana University of Pennsylvania
Indiana, PA 15705

One more thing: I am from Slovakia, but I speak English.

UNIT 21

1 PRE-READING

A **Look at the picture. Answer the questions.**

1. Where do you think this village is?
2. Why do people sometimes visit villages like this one?

B **Read the title of the story. Look at the picture again. Answer the questions.**

1. What do you think this story is about?
2. Can you guess what happens?

The Two Lives of Mary Sutton

Do you believe in reincarnation—that you lived before? Jenny Cockell does. Jenny is a doctor who lives in England. She is married and has two children. That is Jenny's present life. Jenny believes that she also had a past life. She believes she was Mary Sutton, an Irish woman who died in 1932.

When Jenny was four years old, she began dreaming about a woman named Mary. She had the same dreams again and again. In one dream, the woman was standing on a beach and looking at the ocean. She seemed to be waiting for someone. In one terrible dream, the woman was lying in bed in a white room. She was dying.

Sometimes in her dreams Jenny saw the woman's village. Jenny thought that it was on the coast of Ireland. Often she looked at a map of Ireland and read the names of villages on the coast. One name—Malahide—seemed familiar. Jenny thought that maybe Malahide was the woman's village.

Jenny dreamed about Mary and Mary's village all her life. Finally, when she was 36 years old, she decided to travel to Ireland. She wanted to see Malahide.

When Jenny arrived in Malahide, she knew immediately that it was the village in her dreams. The streets, the shops, and the churches all looked familiar. She was in Mary's village!

Jenny decided to look for Mary's little house. She had seen it often in her dreams. It was on a narrow road south of the village. Jenny walked to the south end of the village and found a narrow road. She walked down the road, but there was no house. There was only an old barn.

When Jenny got back to England, she wrote a letter to the man who owned the barn. "Was there ever a small house near your barn?" she asked him.

"Yes," the man wrote back. "There was once a small house near the barn. A family with six children lived there. The mother died in childbirth in 1932. Her name was Mary Sutton."

Jenny found out that after Mary died, Mary's husband couldn't take care of their children. He gave them to other people, and they grew up apart. Jenny decided to find Mary's children. Two of the six children had died, but Jenny found the four surviving children. "Please meet me in Malahide," Jenny wrote them.

In Malahide, Mary's children, who were in their sixties and seventies, told Jenny stories about their childhood.

Sonny, the oldest child, said, "When I was 12, I got a job on an island near Malahide. Every evening a boat brought me home. My mother often waited for me on the beach."

All of the stories seemed familiar to Jenny; she is sure that she is the reincarnation of Mary Sutton. Some of the Sutton children think so, too. Sonny, who is 35 years older than Jenny, says, "To me, she is my mother."

2 VOCABULARY

Complete the sentences with the words below.

barn   childhood   surviving   village

1. Only a few hundred people live in Malahide. It is a ___village___.
2. Jenny walked down a narrow road south of the village, but she saw no house. She saw only a building where animals sleep. She saw a ______________.
3. Two of Mary's six children had died, but Jenny found the four children who were alive. She found the ______________ children.
4. The Sutton children told Jenny about the time when they were children in Malahide. They told stories about their ______________.

3 COMPREHENSION

UNDERSTANDING THE MAIN IDEAS

Circle the letter of the best answer.

1. Jenny believes she is the reincarnation of Mary Sutton because
   a. Mary Sutton was her grandmother.
   b. she saw Mary's life in her dreams.
   c. most people in England believe in reincarnation.
2. Jenny's dreams gave her a lot of information about Mary's life. All of the information was
   a. wonderful.
   b. sad.
   c. correct.

FINDING MORE INFORMATION

Read each sentence on the left. Which sentence on the right gives you more information? Write the letter of the answer on the line.

__e__ 1. Jenny Cockell has a present life.
____ 2. Jenny believes she also had a past life.
____ 3. Jenny had the same dreams again and again.
____ 4. In her dreams, Jenny saw the woman's village.
____ 5. Jenny looked for Mary's house.
____ 6. Jenny looked for Mary's children.

a. It was on the coast of Ireland, and its name was Malahide.
b. She believes she was Mary Sutton, an Irish woman who died in 1932.
c. In one dream, a woman was standing on a beach.
d. It was on a narrow road south of the village.
e. She is a doctor who lives in England.
f. They were in their 60s and 70s.

REMEMBERING DETAILS

Read each sentence. If the sentence describes Jenny Cockell, write a *J* for Jenny. If the sentence describes Mary Sutton, write an *M* for Mary.

__J__ 1. She lives in England.
____ 2. She lived in Ireland.
____ 3. She had six children.
____ 4. She often looked at maps of Ireland.
____ 5. She has two children.
____ 6. Her son worked on an island.
____ 7. She dreamed about a woman.
____ 8. She lived in a little house on a narrow road.

4 DISCUSSION

Jenny dreamed about a woman named Mary all her life. After Jenny traveled to Malahide, Ireland, she was sure she was the reincarnation of Mary Sutton.

A **Check (✓) your answers to the questions below.**

1. Do you believe that Jenny Cockell is the reincarnation of Mary Sutton?
   - ☐ Yes
   - ☐ No
   - ☐ Maybe
2. Do you believe that you have a past life—that you lived before?
   - ☐ Yes
   - ☐ No
   - ☐ Maybe
3. Do you believe that your dreams are important?
   - ☐ Yes
   - ☐ No
   - ☐ Maybe

B **Explain your answers in a small group.**

5 WRITING

When Jenny was in Malahide, she kept a diary. She wrote down everything she saw and did. Complete Jenny's diary.

June 3

When I arrived in Malahide, I went to a small hotel in the center of the village. After I unpacked my suitcase, I ate lunch at the hotel. Then I went outside to look around the village . . .

____
____
____
____
____
____
____

UNIT 22

Wesley Autrey

1 PRE-READING

A **Look at the picture. Answer the questions.**

1. The man in the photo is Wesley Autrey. Where is he standing?
2. How do you think he feels?

B **Read the title of the story. Look at the drawing on this page. Answer the questions.**

1. Where do you think the two strangers met?
2. What do you think this story is about?
3. Can you guess what happens?

Two Strangers

One afternoon Wesley Autrey and his two young daughters, ages four and six, were standing on a subway platform in New York City. Wesley was a construction worker on the second shift. He was taking his daughters home from school before he went to work.

A young man was standing nearby. He was Cameron Peters, a 20-year-old student. Suddenly Cameron began to shake all over and fell to the ground. He had epilepsy, and he was having a seizure. Wesley knew first aid, so he ran to help Cameron. He put a pen between Cameron's teeth so he wouldn't bite his tongue. Then he waited for Cameron to stop shaking. When the seizure was over, Cameron stood up. "Are you all right?" Wesley asked him. "Yes, I'm fine," Cameron answered.

Wesley was walking away when Cameron had another seizure. He fell to the ground again, but this time he fell off the subway platform and onto the tracks below. Wesley looked into the tunnel at the end of the station and saw two white lights. A train was coming. "Hold on to my daughters," Wesley yelled to two women who were standing on the platform. Then he jumped down onto the tracks.

Wesley tried to lift Cameron and put him back on the platform, but he couldn't. Cameron was heavier than he was, and the platform was four feet above the tracks. Wesley looked into the tunnel again. The two white lights were much closer now. The train was coming into the station.

Wesley looked down and saw that there was a space between the tracks about 22 inches deep. As a construction worker, Wesley often worked in small spaces. "I think we can both fit," he decided. He pushed Cameron into the space between the tracks. Then he lay down on top of him. "Don't move," Wesley said, "or one of us is going to lose a leg."

The driver of the train saw the two men on the tracks and put on the brakes. But he wasn't able to stop the train in time. When the first car of the train went over Wesley and Cameron, it moved Wesley's hat a little. Wesley put his head down further, and four more cars went over them. When the train stopped, Wesley and Cameron were under the fifth car. Wesley could hear people on the platform screaming. "We're okay down here," he yelled, "but I've got two daughters up there. Let them know their father's okay."

Paramedics arrived and helped Wesley and Cameron out from under the train. They were both fine.

Cameron remembers almost nothing about the experience. He doesn't remember falling off the platform, and he doesn't remember the train going over him and Wesley. He remembers waking up after the train stopped and seeing Wesley's face. "Am I dead?" he asked Wesley. "Am I in heaven?"

"No, you're not dead, and you're not in heaven," Wesley answered. "You're alive, and you're under a subway train in New York City."

"Who are you?" Cameron asked, and Wesley answered, "I'm someone who saved your life."

2 VOCABULARY

Which words have the same meaning as the words in *italics*? Write the letter of the answer on the line.

b 1. Cameron was *having a seizure.*

_____ 2. When it was *over*, Cameron stood up.

_____ 3. Wesley knew how to give *first aid.*

_____ 4. Wesley decided, "*We can fit.*"

_____ 5. The driver *wasn't able to* stop.

a. There is enough room.

b. unconscious and shaking

c. couldn't

d. finished

e. medical assistance

3 COMPREHENSION

UNDERSTANDING THE MAIN IDEAS

Complete the sentences. Write the answers on the lines.

1. Wesley and Cameron were standing on a subway platform.
2. When Cameron had the second seizure, he ____________________ off the platform and onto the ____________________ below.
3. Wesley looked into the tunnel and saw two white ____________________.
4. Wesley couldn't put Cameron back on the platform because Cameron was ____________________ than he was, and the platform was four ____________________ above the tracks.
5. Wesley pushed Cameron into the space ____________________ the ____________________.
6. When the first car went over the two men, it moved Wesley's ____________________ a little.
7. When the train stopped, the men were under the ____________________ car.
8. From under the train, Wesley yelled, "Let ____________________ know their father's okay."

UNDERSTANDING TIME RELATIONSHIPS

Find the best way to complete each sentence. Write the letter of the answer on the line.

1. Wesley was walking away b
2. The driver of the train put on the breaks _____
3. Wesley put his head down further _____
4. "We're okay down here," Wesley yelled _____
5. "Am I dead?" Cameron asked Wesley _____

a. when he woke up under the train.
b. when Cameron had another seizure.
c. when he heard people on the platform screaming.
d. when the first car moved his hat a little.
e. when he saw the two men on the tracks.

FINDING INFORMATION

Read each question. Find the answer in the paragraph on the next page and circle it. Write the number of the question above the answer.

1. What is Wesley's last name?
2. How old were his daughters?
3. In what city is the subway platform?
4. What was Wesley's work?
5. When did he work?
6. Where was he taking his daughters?

One afternoon Wesley Autrey [1] and his two young daughters, ages four and six, were standing on a subway platform in New York City. Wesley was a construction worker on the second shift. He was taking his daughters home from school before he went to work.

4 DISCUSSION / WRITING

Many people admire Wesley Autrey: They like him and have a good opinion of him. We admire someone who saves another person's life—especially if the other person is a stranger.

A **What kind of person do you admire? Think of three ways to complete the sentence below. Write your answers on the lines. Then share your answers with the class.**

I admire someone who . . .

____.

____.

____.

B **Write a paragraph about someone you admire. Explain why you admire him or her. Here is what one student wrote.**

I admire my mother because she is a strong woman. My father died when I was four years old, and my mother took care of ten children alone.

ANSWER KEY

UNIT 1

VOCABULARY page 3

2. shivering
3. curious
4. amazed
5. rough

UNDERSTANDING THE MAIN IDEA page 4

1. c 2. b

UNDERSTANDING CAUSE AND EFFECT page 4

2. d 3. b 4. a 5. e

REVIEWING THE STORY page 4

2. came
3. was
4. followed
5. swim
6. girlfriend
7. about
8. distance
9. rough
10. famous
11. love

UNIT 2

VOCABULARY page 7

2. trick
3. courthouse
4. shake
5. wedding

UNDERSTANDING THE MAIN IDEA page 8

1. c 2. b

UNDERSTANDING CONNECTIONS page 8

2. d 3. a 4. c

REMEMBERING DETAILS pages 8–9

2. ~~brothers~~ / parents
3. ~~party~~ / wedding
4. ~~boss~~ / friend
5. ~~Monday~~ / Saturday
6. ~~problem~~ / trick
7. ~~library~~ / courthouse
8. ~~called~~ / saw
9. ~~Bob's~~ / John's
10. ~~boyfriend~~ / husband

UNIT 3

VOCABULARY page 11

2. c 3. a 4. d 5. b

UNDERSTANDING THE MAIN IDEAS page 12

2. b, c
3. a, c
4. a, b
5. a, b
6. b, c

FINDING INFORMATION pages 12–13

2. two grown children
3. Sally
4. The next day
5. $23,000
6. on the coast of England
7. at all the best restaurants
8. expensive gifts for his family and friends

UNDERSTANDING A SUMMARY page 13

2

UNIT 4

VOCABULARY page 15

2. stare
3. got tired
4. argued

UNDERSTANDING THE MAIN IDEAS page 16

1. c 2. b

REMEMBERING DETAILS page 16

2. ~~doctors~~ / twins
3. ~~laugh~~ / stare
4. ~~Australian~~ / American
5. ~~days~~ / years
6. ~~cousins~~ / sisters
7. ~~unhappy~~ / happy
8. ~~can~~ / can't

UNDERSTANDING REASONS page 16

2. d 3. b 4. a 5. c

UNIT 5

VOCABULARY page 19

2. b 3. a 4. a

UNDERSTANDING THE MAIN IDEAS page 20

1. b 2. c 3. a

UNDERSTANDING CAUSE AND EFFECT page 20

2. c 3. d 4. a 5. b

UNDERSTANDING A SUMMARY page 20

1

UNIT 6

VOCABULARY page 23

2. widower
3. searched
4. spotted

UNDERSTANDING A SUMMARY page 24

A
1. police
2. night, quiet
3. living, watch
4. gone, grandson
5. bought, tape

B Correct order of the sentences: 2, 5, 1, 3, 4

UNDERSTANDING QUOTATIONS page 24

2. d 3. e 4. a 5. b

REMEMBERING DETAILS page 25

A
2. He is a widower.
4. He lives alone.
5. He has a daughter.
6. He had trouble sleeping.
8. He is a grandfather.

B
1. It sounded like a ghost or a child.
3. Alfred heard it every night for 15 seconds.
4. It said, "Come and catch me."
5. It repeated the sentence five times.
7. It woke Alfred up.
8. It came from a watch.

UNIT 7

VOCABULARY pages 27–28

2. aerial
3. zoomed in
4. familiar
5. vacant

UNDERSTANDING PLACE page 28

3 Saroo grew up happy and healthy.
1 Saroo and his brother looked for money under train seats.
2 Saroo lived on the streets.
1 Saroo got on a train to look for his brother.
3 Saroo looked at aerial photos of earth.
1 Saroo walked to his old house.
2 Someone took Saroo to a home for children with no parents.

FINDING MORE INFORMATION page 28

2. e 3. d 4. a 5. b

LOOKING FOR INFORMATION pages 28–29

2. Fourteen hours
3. Kolkata
4. 1,600 kilometers
5. For three weeks
6. "What's your name?" "Where are you from?"
7. he didn't know his last name or the name of his city
8. in Australia

UNIT 8

VOCABULARY page 31

2. narrow
3. drill
4. rushed
5. injured

UNDERSTANDING THE MAIN IDEAS page 32

1. b 2. c

UNDERSTANDING TIME RELATIONSHIPS page 32

2. c 3. e 4. a 5. b

REMEMBERING DETAILS pages 32–33

2. ~~kitchen~~ / yard
3. ~~water~~ / well
4. ~~wrote~~ / dialed
5. ~~cover~~ / hole
6. ~~soft~~ / solid
7. ~~down~~ / up
8. ~~doctors~~ / paramedics
9. ~~old~~ / young
10. ~~days~~ / hours

WRITING page 33

Jessica was playing at a daycare center. Suddenly she fell into a well. She fell about 20 feet and couldn't get out of the well.

Men from the fire department came. They couldn't go down into the well because it was too narrow. The men decided to drill a hole next to the well.

For the next 58 hours the men drilled the hole. Their job was very difficult because they were drilling through solid rock. Finally they reached Jessica and brought her up from the well. Jessica's foot and forehead were badly injured, but she was alive. Everyone was very happy.

UNIT 9

VOCABULARY page 35

2. tank
3. success
4. order
5. change

REVIEWING THE STORY page 36

2. owner
3. drove
4. business
5. money
6. bills
7. fast-food
8. more
9. forward

UNDERSTANDING CAUSE AND EFFECT page 36

2. e 3. a 4. d 5. c

FINDING INFORMATION pages 36–37

2. 22
3. For weeks
4. In a small town in Mississippi
5. He couldn't pay for a hotel room
6. For two days
7. Early in the morning
8. Only one man
9. a big breakfast
10. "I lost my wallet!"

UNIT 10

VOCABULARY page 39

2. strange
3. ingredients
4. dried
5. common

UNDERSTANDING THE MAIN IDEAS page 40

1. b 2. b 3. c

REMEMBERING DETAILS page 40

2. f 3. d 4. a 5. b 6. e

FINDING MORE INFORMATION page 40

2. a 3. c 4. b

UNIT 11

VOCABULARY page 43

2. d 3. e 4. a 5. c

UNDERSTANDING CONNECTIONS page 44

2. d 3. a 4. f 5. c 6. e

MAKING INFERENCES page 44

2. d 3. a 4. c

UNDERSTANDING A SUMMARY page 44

2

UNIT 12

VOCABULARY page 47

2. ripped
3. slammed on their brakes
4. grabbed

REMEMBERING DETAILS page 48

2. ~~bus~~ / truck
3. ~~closed~~ / opened
4. ~~paper~~ / plastic
5. ~~leaves~~ / money
6. ~~houses~~ / cars
7. ~~30~~ / 20
8. ~~tax~~ / reward
9. ~~pennies~~ / dollars

UNDERSTANDING TIME RELATIONSHIPS page 48

2. b 3. a 4. e 5. d

MAKING INFERENCES page 48

2. a 3. e 4. d 5. c

UNIT 13

VOCABULARY page 51

2. b 3. f 4. d 5. a 6. c

REMEMBERING DETAILS page 52

~~fruit~~ / flea
~~new~~ / used
~~dessert~~ / dinner
~~weeks~~ / months
~~mind~~ / heart
~~Mexico~~ / Canada
~~$5,000~~ / $55,000
~~car~~ / truck
~~California~~ / Florida
~~55~~ / 105

FINDING MORE INFORMATION page 52

2. a 3. d 4. b

UNDERSTANDING TIME AND PLACE page 53

WHEN	WHERE
at the end of the day	at the flea market
for the next four months	on the way from Indiana to Canada
after they got married	at the hotel
	all over the United States

UNIT 14

VOCABULARY pages 55–56

2. auctioneer
3. chanted
4. offer
5. cheered

REMEMBERING DETAILS page 56

2. ~~Seven~~ / Seventeen
3. ~~December~~ / July
4. ~~world~~ / county
5. ~~lowest~~ / highest
6. ~~cents~~ / dollars
7. ~~auctioneer~~ / farmer
8. ~~thanked~~ /paid

UNDERSTANDING CAUSE AND EFFECT page 56

2. d 3. a 4. b 5. c

UNDERSTANDING A SUMMARY page 57

2

UNIT 15

VOCABULARY pages 59–60

2. refund
3. set the timer
4. experts
5. teller

REMEMBERING DETAILS page 60

2. She washed it with her jeans.
3. She put it on the kitchen table to dry.
5. She burned it in her microwave oven.
6. She showed it to a teller at the bank.
7. She sent it to the Treasury Department.
9. She gave it to friends.

UNDERSTANDING PRONOUNS page 60

2. c 3. h 4. d 5. e 6. f 7. a 8. g

UNDERSTANDING A SUMMARY page 61

2

UNIT 16

VOCABULARY page 63

2. a 3. c 4. b

UNDERSTANDING THE MAIN IDEAS page 64

1. Mendez
2. farmer, farm worker
3. children, elementary
4. old
5. fight, school
6. close
7. lawyer, court
8. separate, unfair

UNDERSTANDING PRONOUNS page 64

2. d 3. c 4. b 5. e

FINDING INFORMATION page 65

2. when he was a little boy
3. at age ten
4. to become a farm worker
5. Felicitas
6. three
7. a small but successful café
8. in Santa Ana, California

UNIT 17

VOCABULARY page 67

2. nets
3. raw
4. survive
5. ran out of

UNDERSTANDING THE MAIN IDEAS page 68

2. b, c
3. a, b
4. a, c
5. a, b
6. a, b

UNDERSTANDING REASONS page 68

2. d 3. e 4. c 5. a

UNDERSTANDING A SUMMARY page 69

2

UNIT 18

VOCABULARY pages 71–72

2. a 3. a 4. a

UNDERSTANDING THE MAIN IDEAS page 72

2. b, c
3. a, b
4. a, b
5. b, c

UNDERSTANDING TIME RELATIONSHIPS page 72

2. d 3. c 4. a 5. b

UNDERSTANDING A SUMMARY page 73

1

UNIT 19

VOCABULARY pages 75–76

2. technician
3. What if
4. damage
5. don't mind

UNDERSTANDING THE MAIN IDEAS page 76

2. a 3. b

REMEMBERING DETAILS pages 76–77

A

2. She usually lives a quiet life.
3. She lives in a suburb of Washington, D.C.
5. She is 75 years old.
7. She has a bad heart.
8. She has a basement in her house.

B

1. On Monday she waited all day for the technician, but he didn't come.
2. The technician disconnected her old phone service, but he couldn't connect her new service.
4. Mona waited for two hours to talk to the manager.
6. A company representative told Mona, "Someone will come to your house next Tuesday," but nobody came.

UNDERSTANDING WORD GROUPS page 77

lamp cook teacher

UNIT 20

VOCABULARY pages 79–80

2. b 3. b 4. a 5. a

UNDERSTANDING THE MAIN IDEAS page 80

1. b 2. b

REMEMBERING DETAILS page 80

2. ~~fish~~ / mermaid
3. ~~Arizona~~ / California
4. ~~south~~ / east
5. ~~years~~ / days
6. ~~mountain~~ / lake
7. ~~feeding~~ / hunting
8. ~~cake~~ / present

FINDING MORE INFORMATION page 81

2. c 3. a 4. d

UNIT 21

VOCABULARY page 83

2. barn
3. surviving
4. childhood

UNDERSTANDING THE MAIN IDEAS page 84

1. b   2. c

FINDING MORE INFORMATION page 84

2. b   3. c   4. a   5. d   6. f

REMEMBERING DETAILS page 84

2. M   3. M   4. J   5. J   6. M   7. J   8. M

UNIT 22

VOCABULARY page 87

2. d   3. e   4. a   5. c

UNDERSTANDING THE MAIN IDEAS page 88

2. fell, tracks
3. lights
4. heavier, feet
5. between, tracks
6. hat
7. fifth
8. them

UNDERSTANDING TIME RELATIONSHIPS page 88

2. e   3. d   4. c   5. a

FINDING INFORMATION pages 88–89

2. four and six
3. New York City
4. construction worker
5. on the second shift
6. home from school

CREDITS

PHOTO CREDITS

Page 2: Damedeeso/123RF; **5:** Alex Staroseltsev/Shutterstock; **6:** Majlan/Shutterstock; **10:** Lucky Business/Shutterstock; **14:** Hulton Deutsch/Corbis Historical/Getty Images; **18:** Randy Duchaine/Alamy Stock Photo; **22:** Motortion Films/Shutterstock; **26:** Shyamalamuralinath/Shutterstock; **28:** Seeyah panwan/Shutterstock; **30:** Bettmann/Getty Images; **34:** Pamela Eldridge/Design Pics Inc/Alamy Stock Photo; **38:** Kostrez/123RF; **41:** Syda Productions/Shutterstock; **42:** Barbara Alper/Archive Photos/Getty Images; **46:** Epic Cure/Shutterstock; **50:** Matyas Rehak/Shutterstock; **54:** Katelizabeth Photography/Alamy Stock Photo; **58:** Joel Sartore/National Geographic Creative/Alamy Stock Photo; **62:** Nature and Science/Alamy Stock Photo; **66:** © Peter Serling, 2018; **70:** STR/AFP/Getty Images; **74:** Richard A. Lipski/The Washington Post/Getty Images; **78:** Matteo Provendola/Shutterstock, *(emoji/icons on balloon)* Notkoo/Shutterstock; **82:** Emily C. McCormick/Shutterstock; **86:** Ron Antonelli/New York Daily News/Getty Images.